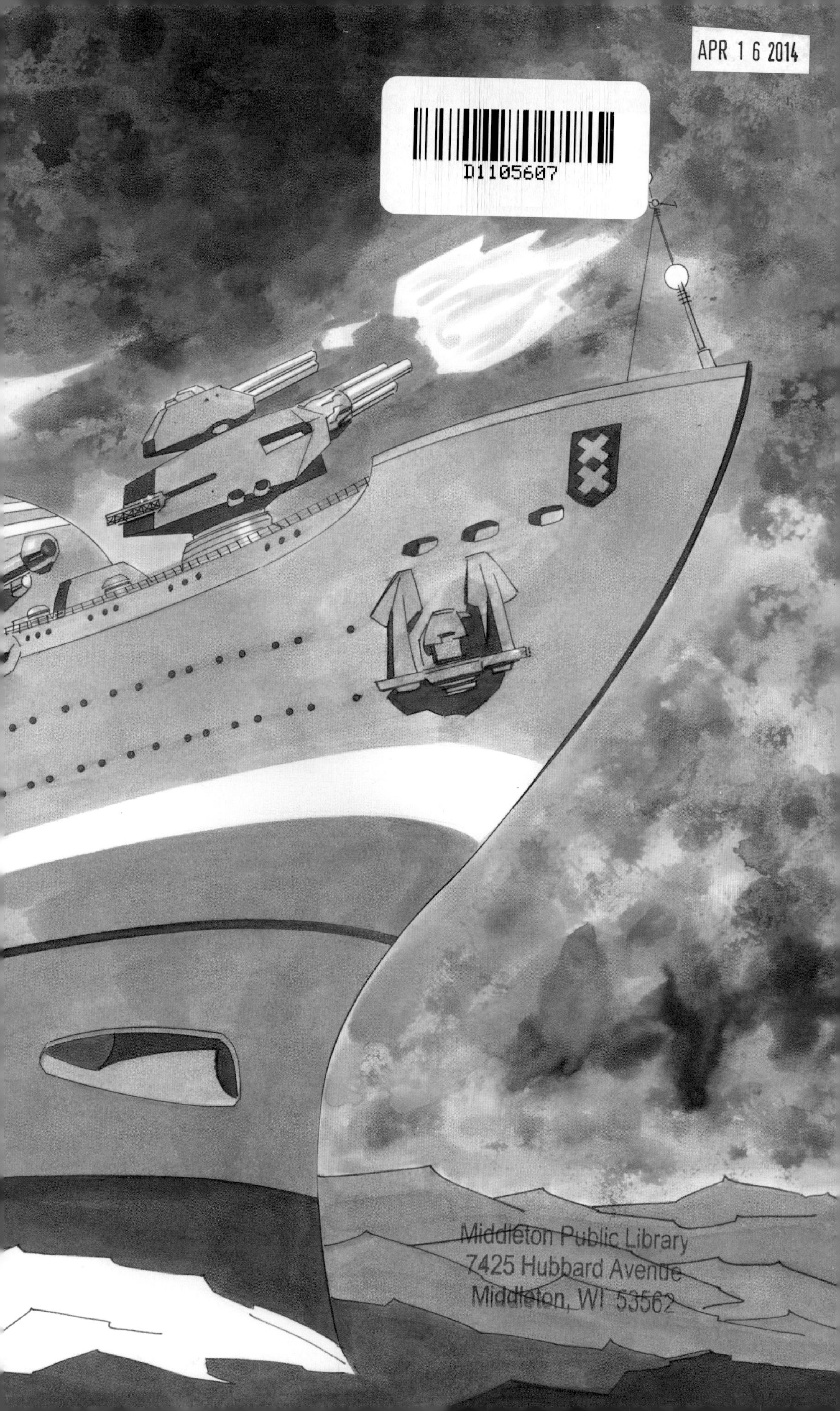

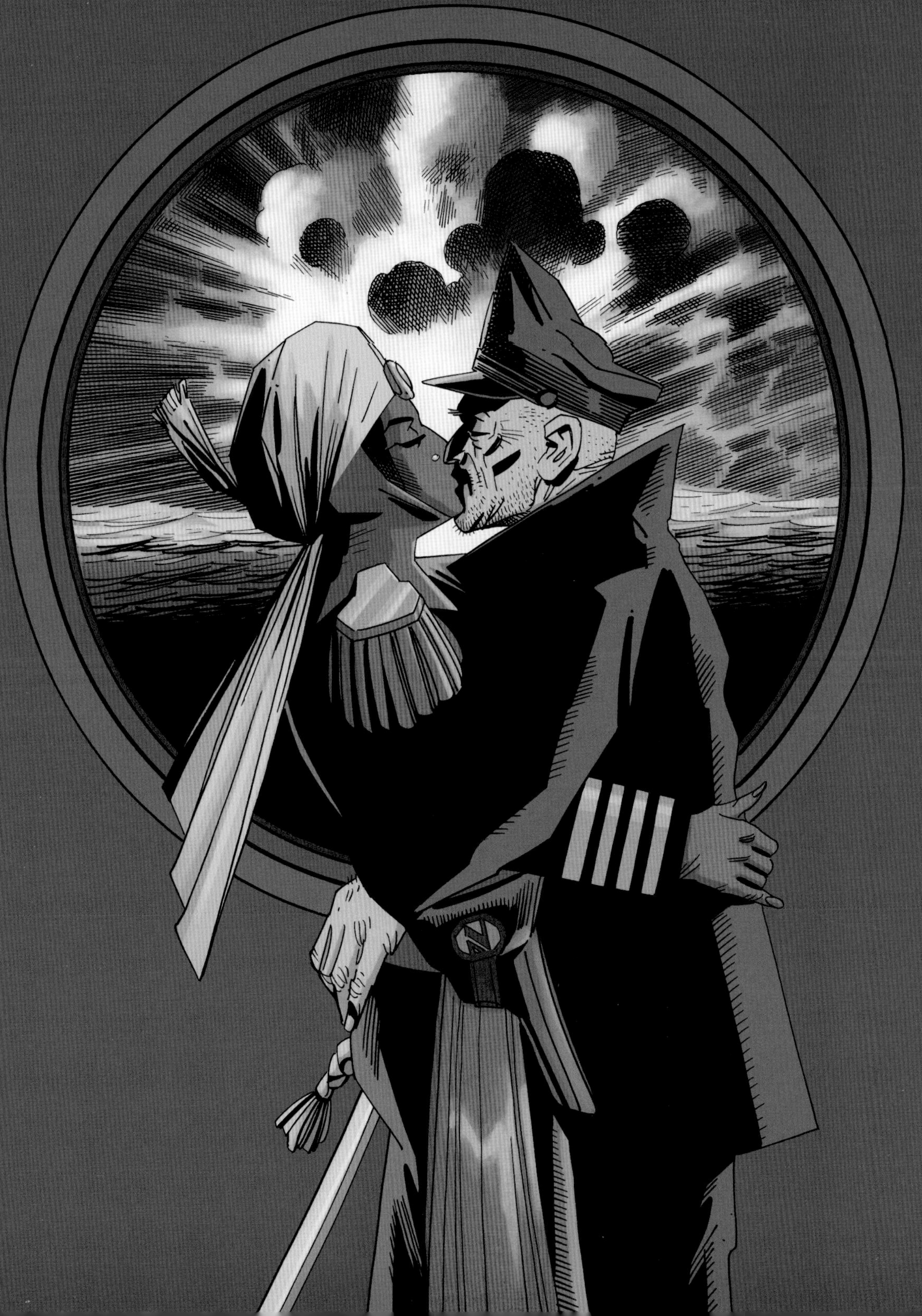

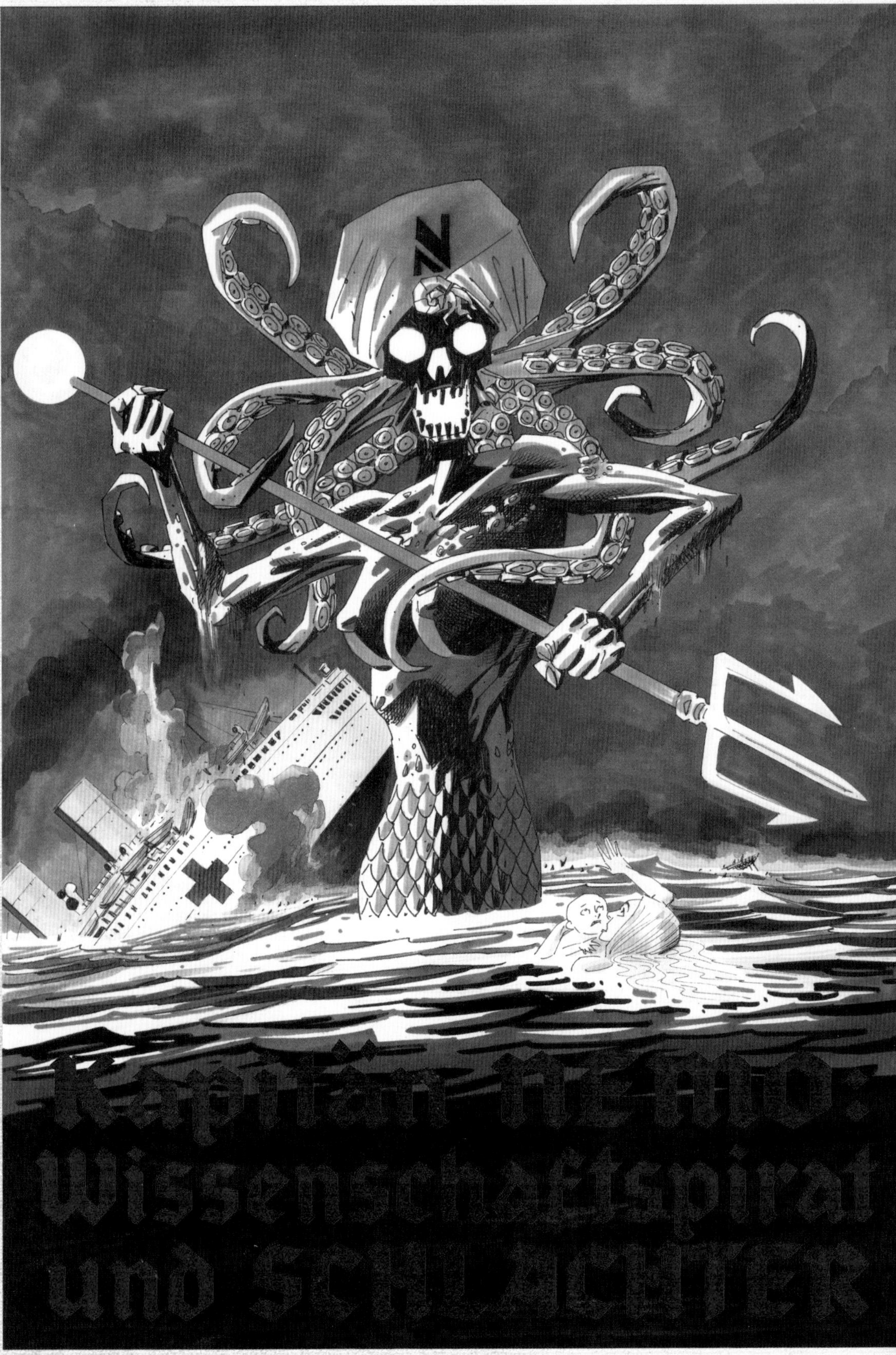
N
Kapitän NEMO:
Wissenschaftspirat
und SCHLACHTER

MINISTRY ⚜ OF WAR
Allied Forces Military Tribunal Charge Sheet

Major Alan Moore – King's Own Heavy Typewriters

> CHARGE: Dereliction of chin while on active service.

Captain Kevin O'Neill – Irish Light Housework Cavalry

> CHARGE: Under the influence of 'Funny Papers' (possibly bomb happy)

Sergeant Todd Klein – 1st division Screaming Calligraphers

> CHARGE: Lettering 'Ginger Nuts' on General Montgomery's dress trousers

Colour Sergeant Ben Dimagmaliw – Rainbow Warrior Coalition

> CHARGE: Colour Coordinating Grenades because...'It felt right.'

Privates Josh Palmano & Tony Bennett – Knockabout 3rd Foot and Mouth

Quartermasters Chris Staros & Brett Warnock – Top Shelf Canteen (excused boots)

> CHARGE: Wilful abuse of 'Camp' Newspaper for the purpose of Moral Pollution.

HM Stationery Office - 1941

Nemo: Roses of Berlin © & ™ 2014 Alan Moore & Kevin O'Neill.
Co-published by Top Shelf Productions, PO Box 1282, Marietta, GA 30061-1282, USA & Knockabout Comics, 42c Lancaster Road, London, W11 1QR, United Kingdom. Top Shelf Productions® and the Top Shelf logo are registered trademarks of Top Shelf Productions, Inc. All Rights Reserved. This is a work of fiction. Names, characters, places, and incidents are the products of the author's imagination or are used fictitiously. Any resemblance to actual events, locales, or persons living or dead, is entirely coincidental. No part of this publication may be reproduced without permission, except for small excerpts for purposes of review. First printing, March, 2014. Printed in China.

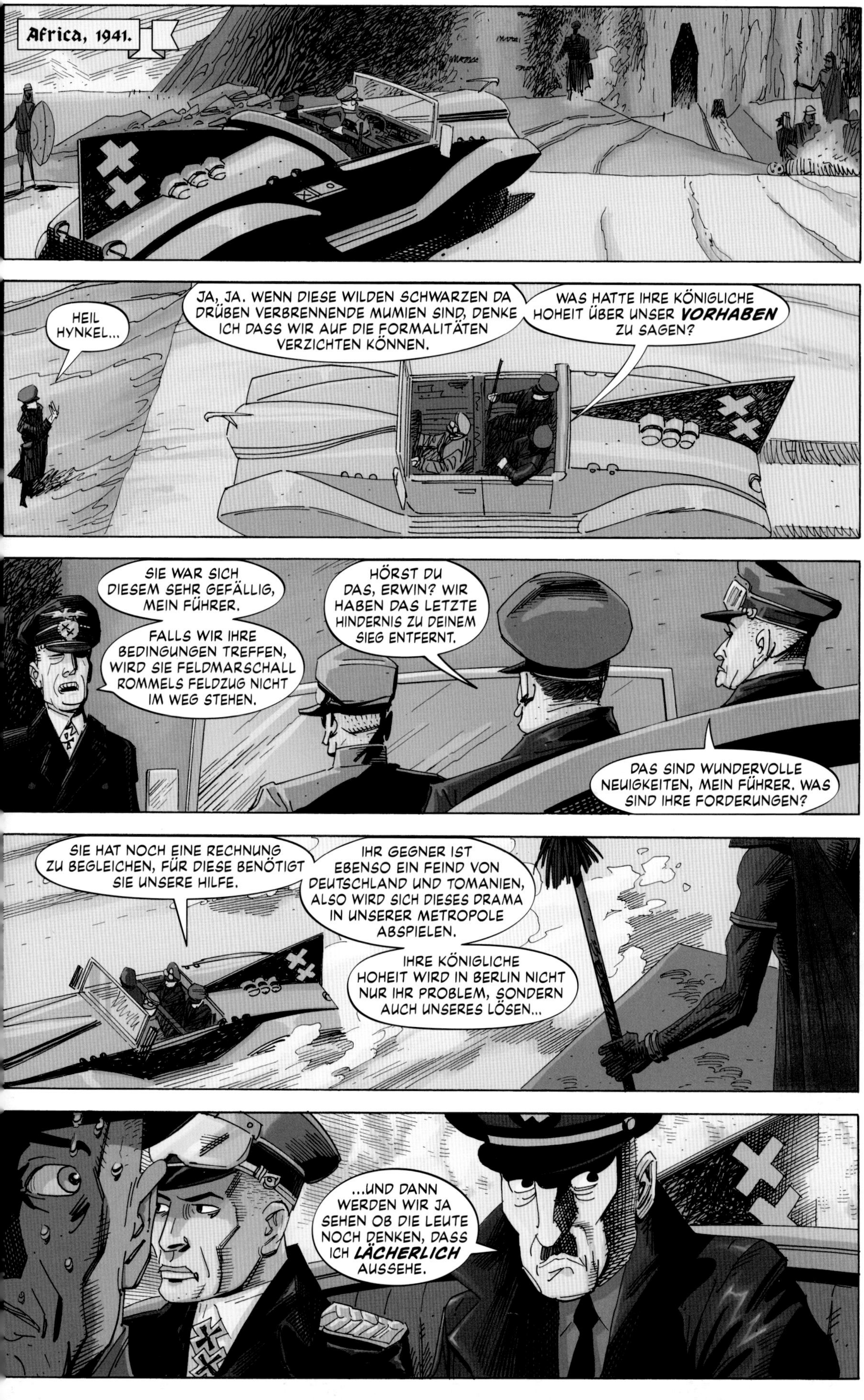
Africa, 1941.
HEIL HYNKEL...
JA, JA. WENN DIESE WILDEN SCHWARZEN DA DRÜBEN VERBRENNENDE MUMIEN SIND, DENKE ICH DASS WIR AUF DIE FORMALITÄTEN VERZICHTEN KÖNNEN.
WAS HATTE IHRE KÖNIGLICHE HOHEIT ÜBER UNSER VORHABEN ZU SAGEN?
SIE WAR SICH DIESEM SEHR GEFÄLLIG, MEIN FÜHRER.
FALLS WIR IHRE BEDINGUNGEN TREFFEN, WIRD SIE FELDMARSCHALL ROMMELS FELDZUG NICHT IM WEG STEHEN.
HÖRST DU DAS, ERWIN? WIR HABEN DAS LETZTE HINDERNIS ZU DEINEM SIEG ENTFERNT.
DAS SIND WUNDERVOLLE NEUIGKEITEN, MEIN FÜHRER. WAS SIND IHRE FORDERUNGEN?
SIE HAT NOCH EINE RECHNUNG ZU BEGLEICHEN, FÜR DIESE BENÖTIGT SIE UNSERE HILFE.
IHR GEGNER IST EBENSO EIN FEIND VON DEUTSCHLAND UND TOMANIEN, ALSO WIRD SICH DIESES DRAMA IN UNSERER METROPOLE ABSPIELEN.
IHRE KÖNIGLICHE HOHEIT WIRD IN BERLIN NICHT NUR IHR PROBLEM, SONDERN AUCH UNSERES LÖSEN...
...UND DANN WERDEN WIR JA SEHEN OB DIE LEUTE NOCH DENKEN, DASS ICH LÄCHERLICH AUSSEHE.

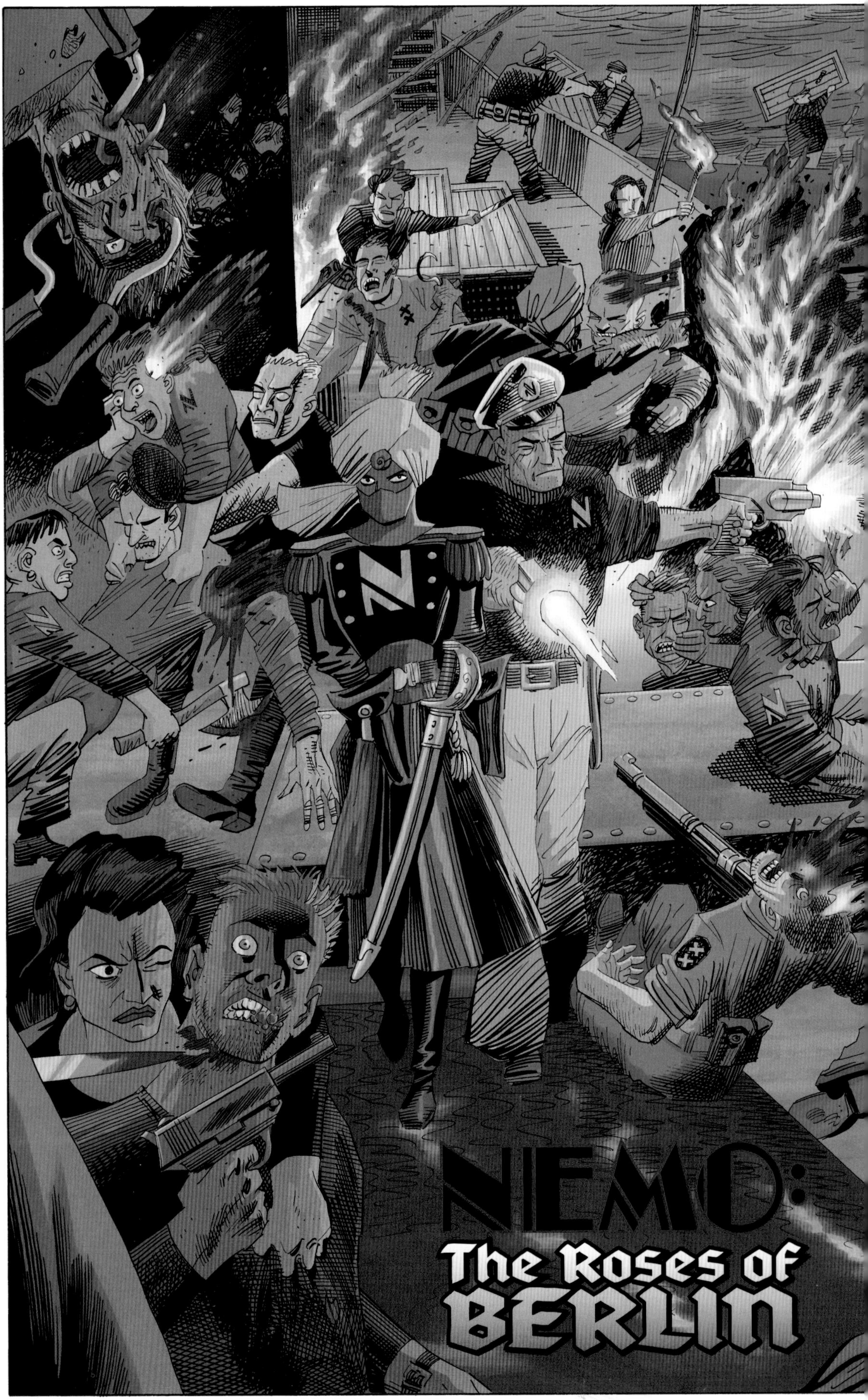
NEMO:
The Roses of
BERLIN

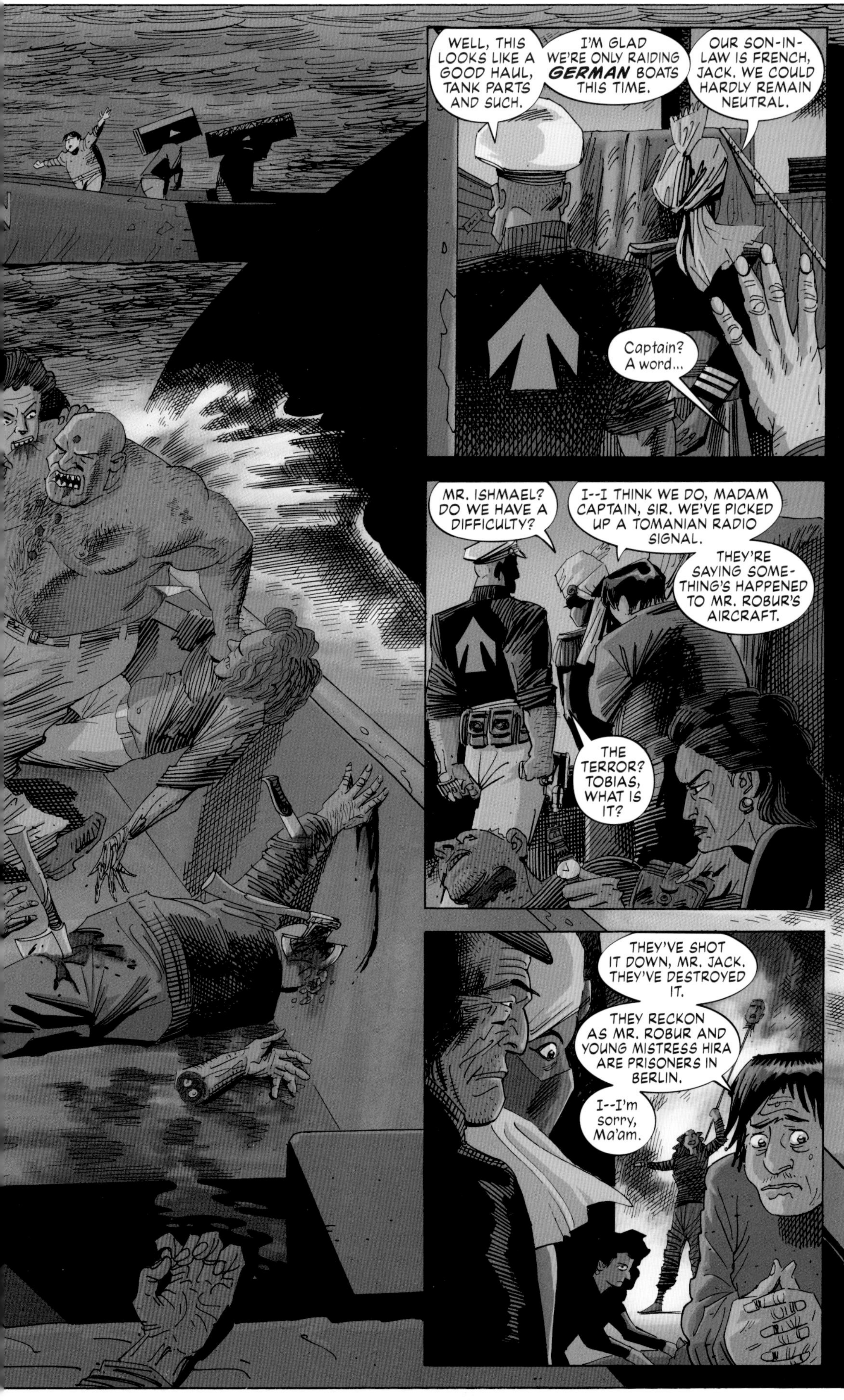

WELL, THIS LOOKS LIKE A GOOD HAUL, TANK PARTS AND SUCH.
I'M GLAD WE'RE ONLY RAIDING GERMAN BOATS THIS TIME.
OUR SON-IN-LAW IS FRENCH, JACK. WE COULD HARDLY REMAIN NEUTRAL.
Captain? A word...
MR. ISHMAEL? DO WE HAVE A DIFFICULTY?
I--I THINK WE DO, MADAM CAPTAIN, SIR. WE'VE PICKED UP A TOMANIAN RADIO SIGNAL.
THEY'RE SAYING SOME-THING'S HAPPENED TO MR. ROBUR'S AIRCRAFT.
THE TERROR? TOBIAS, WHAT IS IT?
THEY'VE SHOT IT DOWN, MR. JACK. THEY'VE DESTROYED IT.
THEY RECKON AS MR. ROBUR AND YOUNG MISTRESS HIRA ARE PRISONERS IN BERLIN.
I--I'm sorry, Ma'am.

JANNI, STRIKING INTO BERLIN...D'YOU NOT THINK WE SHOULD PLAN THIS OUT FIRST?

THEY ARE PROBABLY RAPING AND TORTURING OUR DAUGHTER AT THIS MOMENT.

NO. WE TAKE THE NAUTILOID ALONG THE *ELBE.* WE RETRIEVE HIRA AND ARMAND.

EVERYONE ELSE, WE KILL.

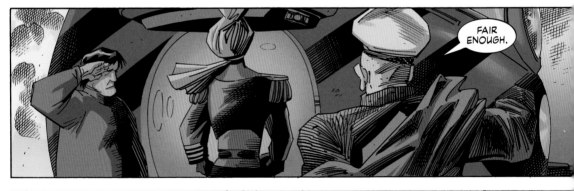

FAIR ENOUGH.

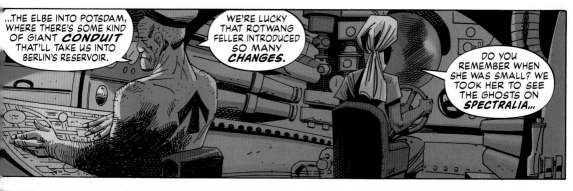

...THE ELBE INTO POTSDAM, WHERE THERE'S SOME KIND OF GIANT *CONDUIT* THAT'LL TAKE US INTO BERLIN'S RESERVOIR.

WE'RE LUCKY THAT ROTWANG FELLER INTRODUCED SO MANY *CHANGES.*

DO YOU REMEMBER WHEN SHE WAS SMALL? WE TOOK HER TO SEE THE GHOSTS ON *SPECTRALIA*...

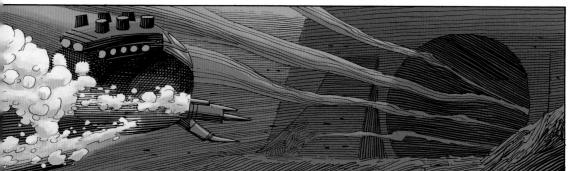

...OPPORTUNITY TO USE THE NEW GUNS. AND THEY WON'T EXPECT US TO RESPOND THIS QUICKLY.

HOW FAR ARE WE FROM THE *CITY?*

HARD TO SAY. THE MARKERS ARE ALL IN ROTWANG'S "BESSERSPRECHT" SYMBOL-LANGUAGE.

WE'RE CLOSE, THOUGH. WE BETTER GET KITTED OUT...

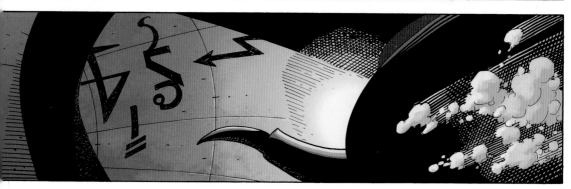

...TIMING, ARRIVING AFTER DARK. ARE YOU SURE YOU'RE READY FOR THIS, DARLIN'?

JACK, WITH OUR DAUGHTER IN THE HANDS OF BUTCHERS, I'M READY FOR ANYTHING.

OPEN THE DOOR AND LET THOSE PAN-GERMANS FACE THE HOUSE OF NEMO WHILE THEY ARE STILL...

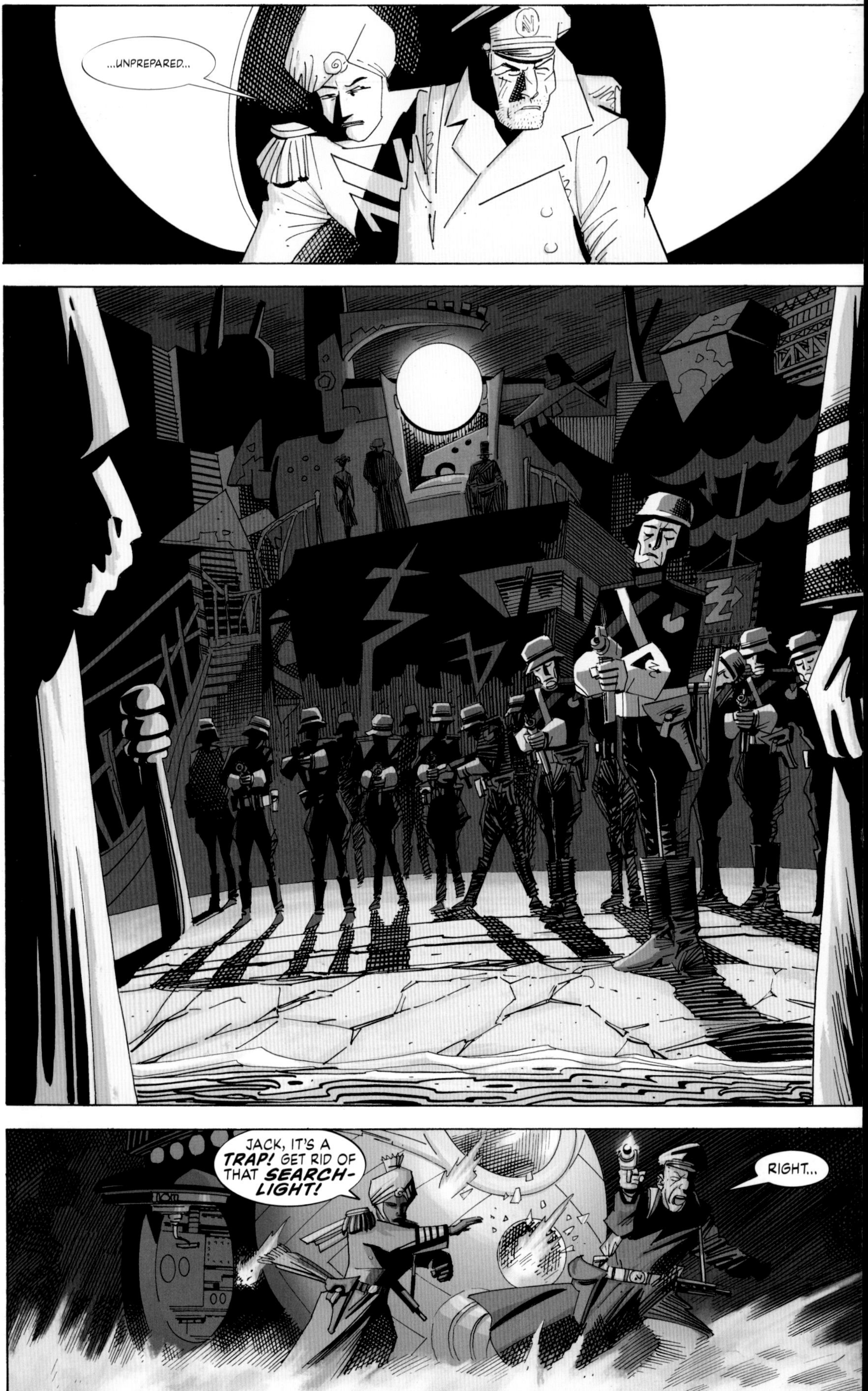
...UNPREPARED...
JACK, IT'S A *TRAP!* GET RID OF THAT *SEARCH-LIGHT!*
RIGHT...

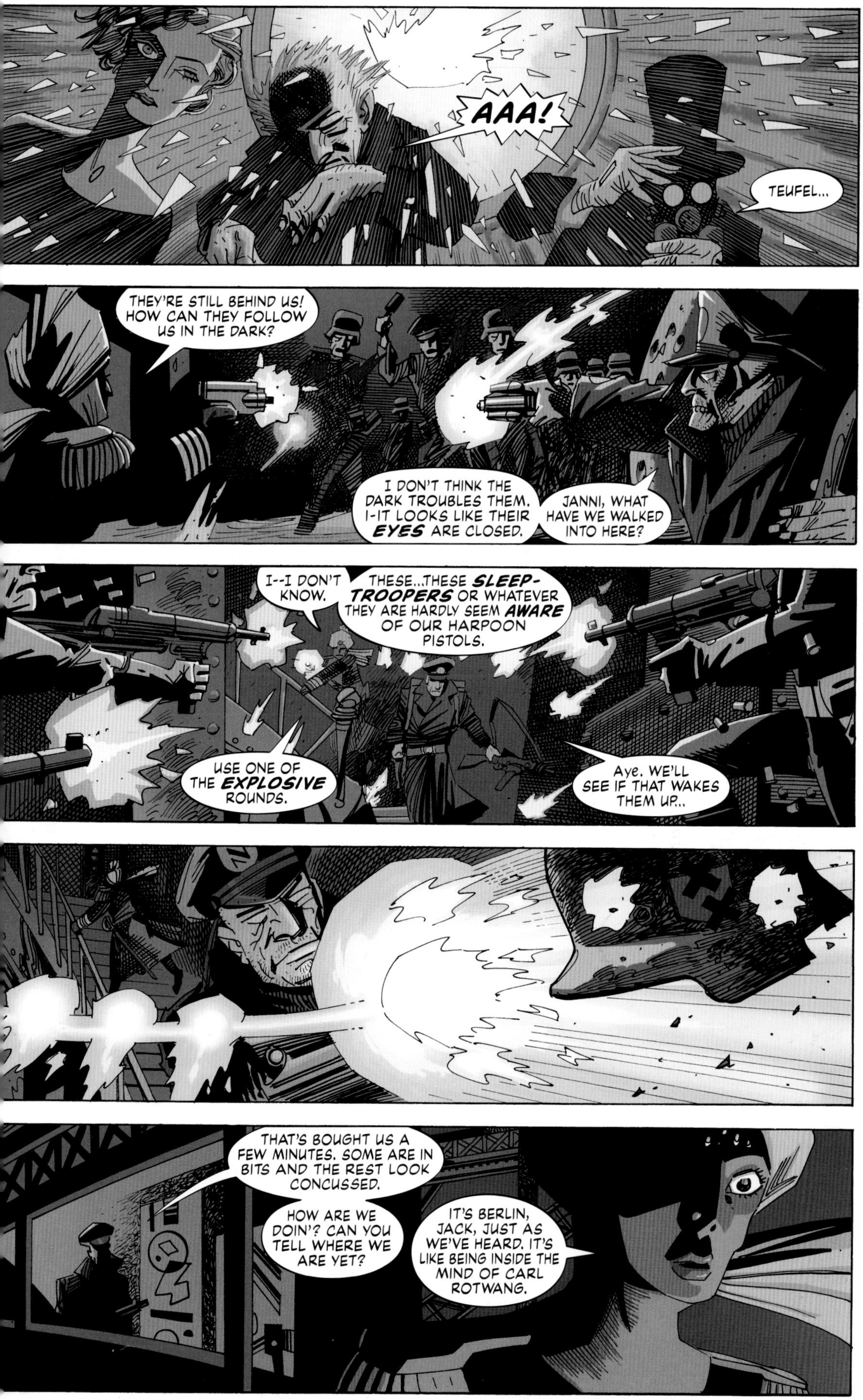
AAA!
TEUFEL...
THEY'RE STILL BEHIND US! HOW CAN THEY FOLLOW US IN THE DARK?
I DON'T THINK THE DARK TROUBLES THEM. I-IT LOOKS LIKE THEIR EYES ARE CLOSED.
JANNI, WHAT HAVE WE WALKED INTO HERE?
I--I DON'T KNOW.
THESE...THESE SLEEP-TROOPERS OR WHATEVER THEY ARE HARDLY SEEM AWARE OF OUR HARPOON PISTOLS.
USE ONE OF THE EXPLOSIVE ROUNDS.
Aye. WE'LL SEE IF THAT WAKES THEM UP...
THAT'S BOUGHT US A FEW MINUTES. SOME ARE IN BITS AND THE REST LOOK CONCUSSED.
HOW ARE WE DOIN'? CAN YOU TELL WHERE WE ARE YET?
IT'S BERLIN, JACK, JUST AS WE'VE HEARD. IT'S LIKE BEING INSIDE THE MIND OF CARL ROTWANG.

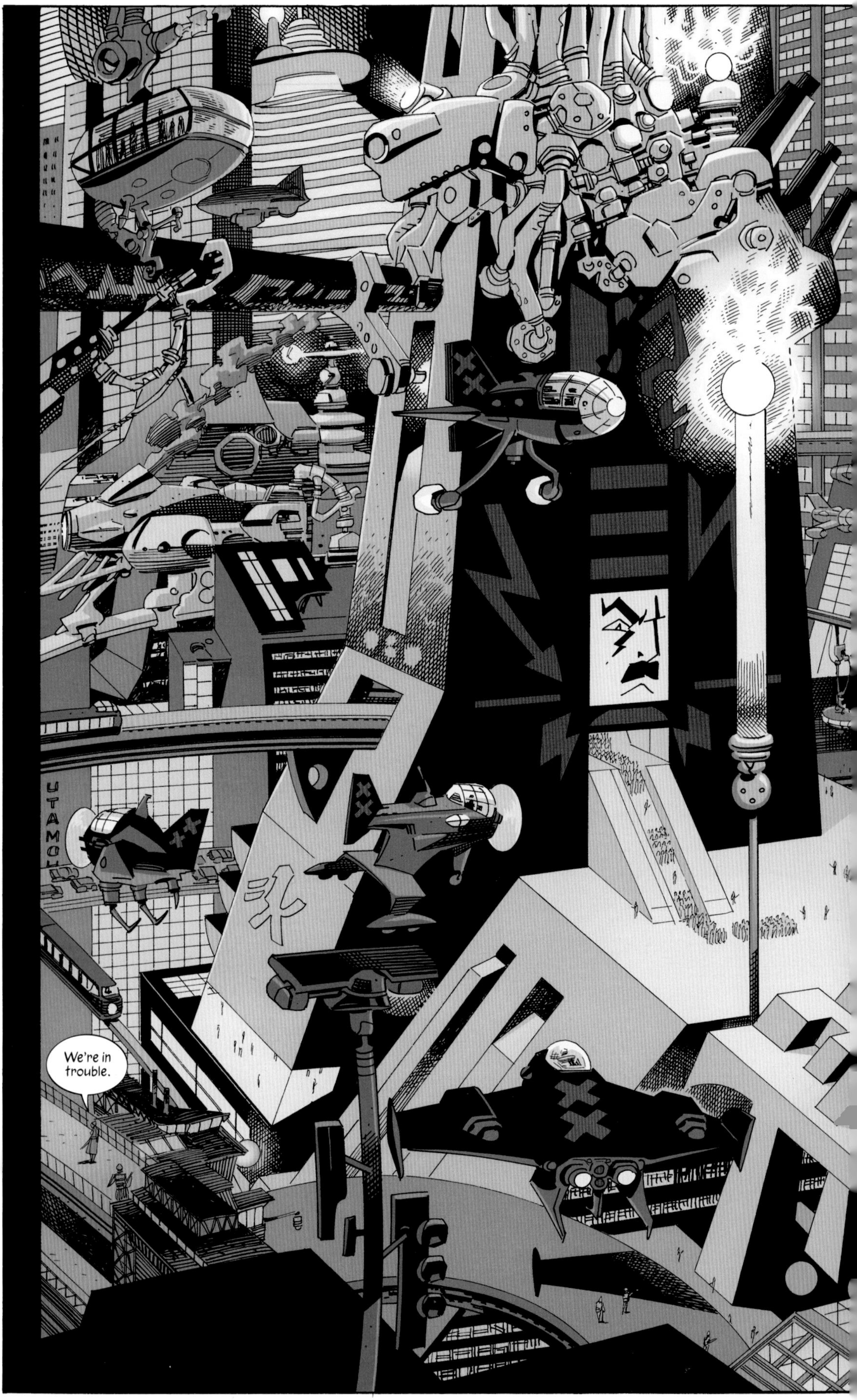
We're in trouble.

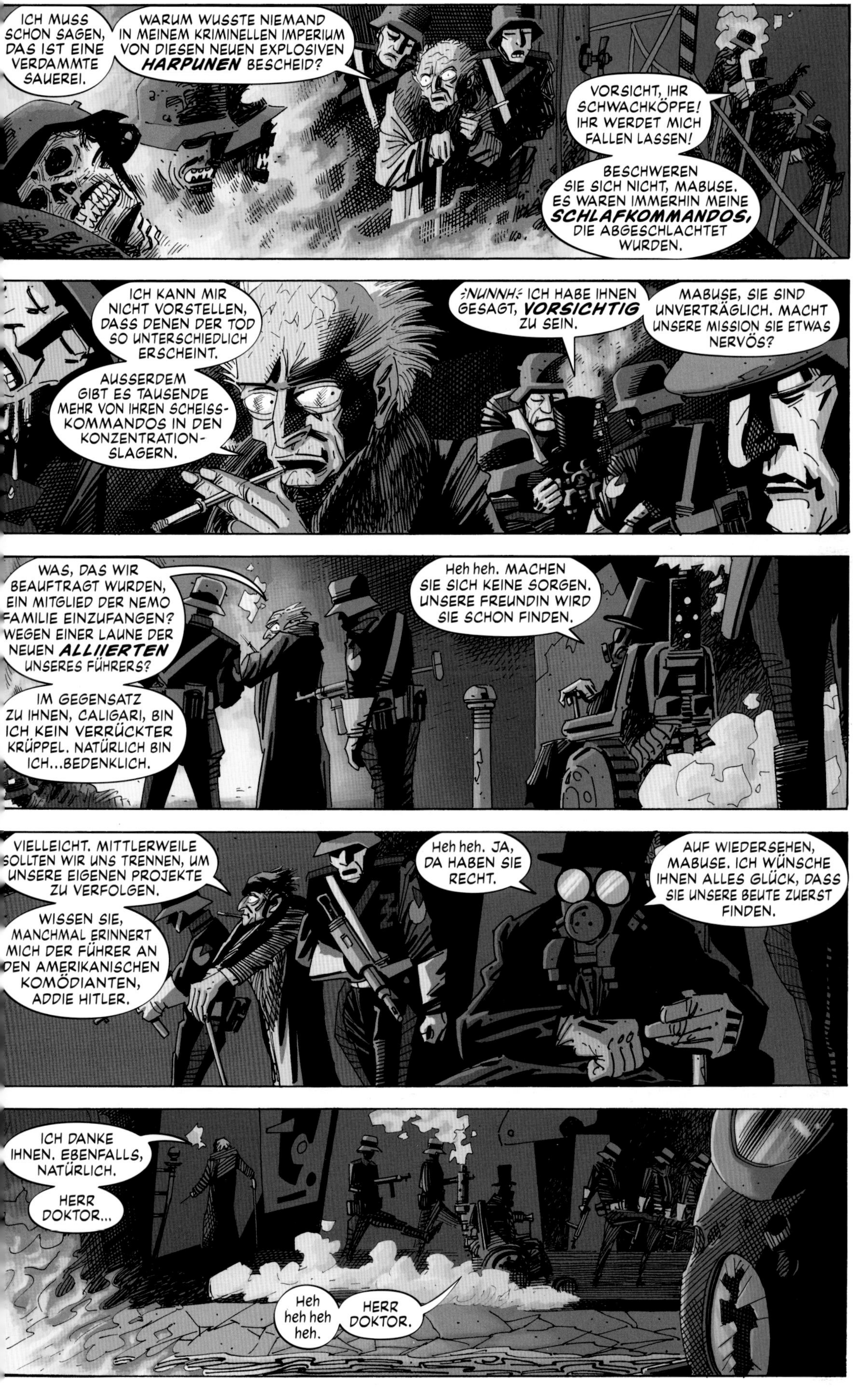
ICH MUSS SCHON SAGEN, DAS IST EINE VERDAMMTE SAUEREI.
WARUM WUSSTE NIEMAND IN MEINEM KRIMINELLEN IMPERIUM VON DIESEN NEUEN EXPLOSIVEN HARPUNEN BESCHEID?
VORSICHT, IHR SCHWACHKÖPFE! IHR WERDET MICH FALLEN LASSEN!
BESCHWEREN SIE SICH NICHT, MABUSE. ES WAREN IMMERHIN MEINE SCHLAFKOMMANDOS, DIE ABGESCHLACHTET WURDEN.
ICH KANN MIR NICHT VORSTELLEN, DASS DENEN DER TOD SO UNTERSCHIEDLICH ERSCHEINT.
AUSSERDEM GIBT ES TAUSENDE MEHR VON IHREN SCHEISS-KOMMANDOS IN DEN KONZENTRATION-SLAGERN.
:NUNNH: ICH HABE IHNEN GESAGT, VORSICHTIG ZU SEIN.
MABUSE, SIE SIND UNVERTRÄGLICH. MACHT UNSERE MISSION SIE ETWAS NERVÖS?
WAS, DAS WIR BEAUFTRAGT WURDEN, EIN MITGLIED DER NEMO FAMILIE EINZUFANGEN? WEGEN EINER LAUNE DER NEUEN ALLIIERTEN UNSERES FÜHRERS?
IM GEGENSATZ ZU IHNEN, CALIGARI, BIN ICH KEIN VERRÜCKTER KRÜPPEL. NATÜRLICH BIN ICH...BEDENKLICH.
Heh heh. MACHEN SIE SICH KEINE SORGEN. UNSERE FREUNDIN WIRD SIE SCHON FINDEN.
VIELLEICHT. MITTLERWEILE SOLLTEN WIR UNS TRENNEN, UM UNSERE EIGENEN PROJEKTE ZU VERFOLGEN.
WISSEN SIE, MANCHMAL ERINNERT MICH DER FÜHRER AN DEN AMERIKANISCHEN KOMÖDIANTEN, ADDIE HITLER.
Heh heh. JA, DA HABEN SIE RECHT.
AUF WIEDERSEHEN, MABUSE. ICH WÜNSCHE IHNEN ALLES GLÜCK, DASS SIE UNSERE BEUTE ZUERST FINDEN.
ICH DANKE IHNEN. EBENFALLS, NATÜRLICH.
HERR DOKTOR...
Heh heh heh heh.
HERR DOKTOR.

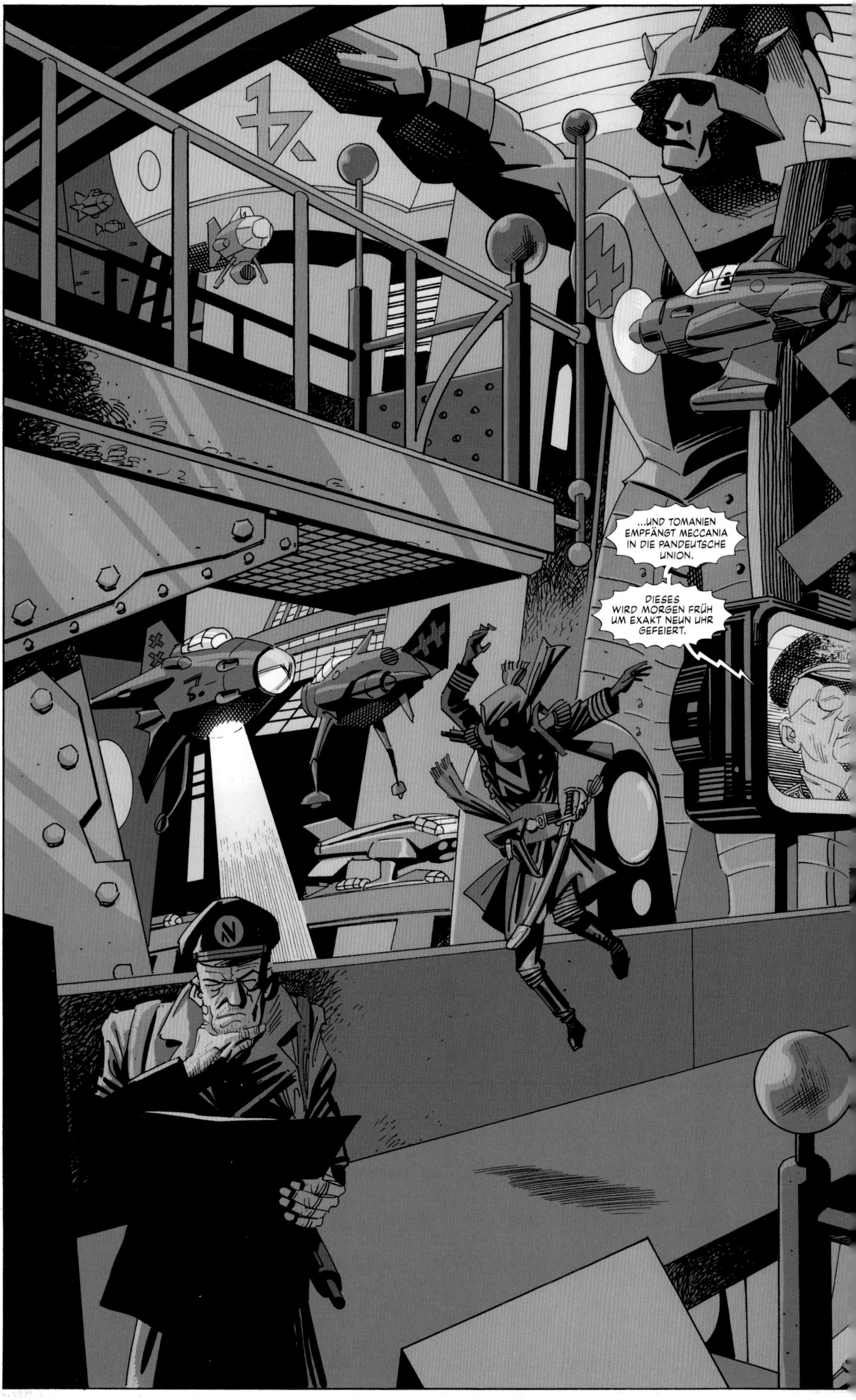
...UND TOMANIEN EMPFÄNGT MECCANIA IN DIE PANDEUTSCHE UNION.
DIESES WIRD MORGEN FRÜH UM EXAKT NEUN UHR GEFEIERT.

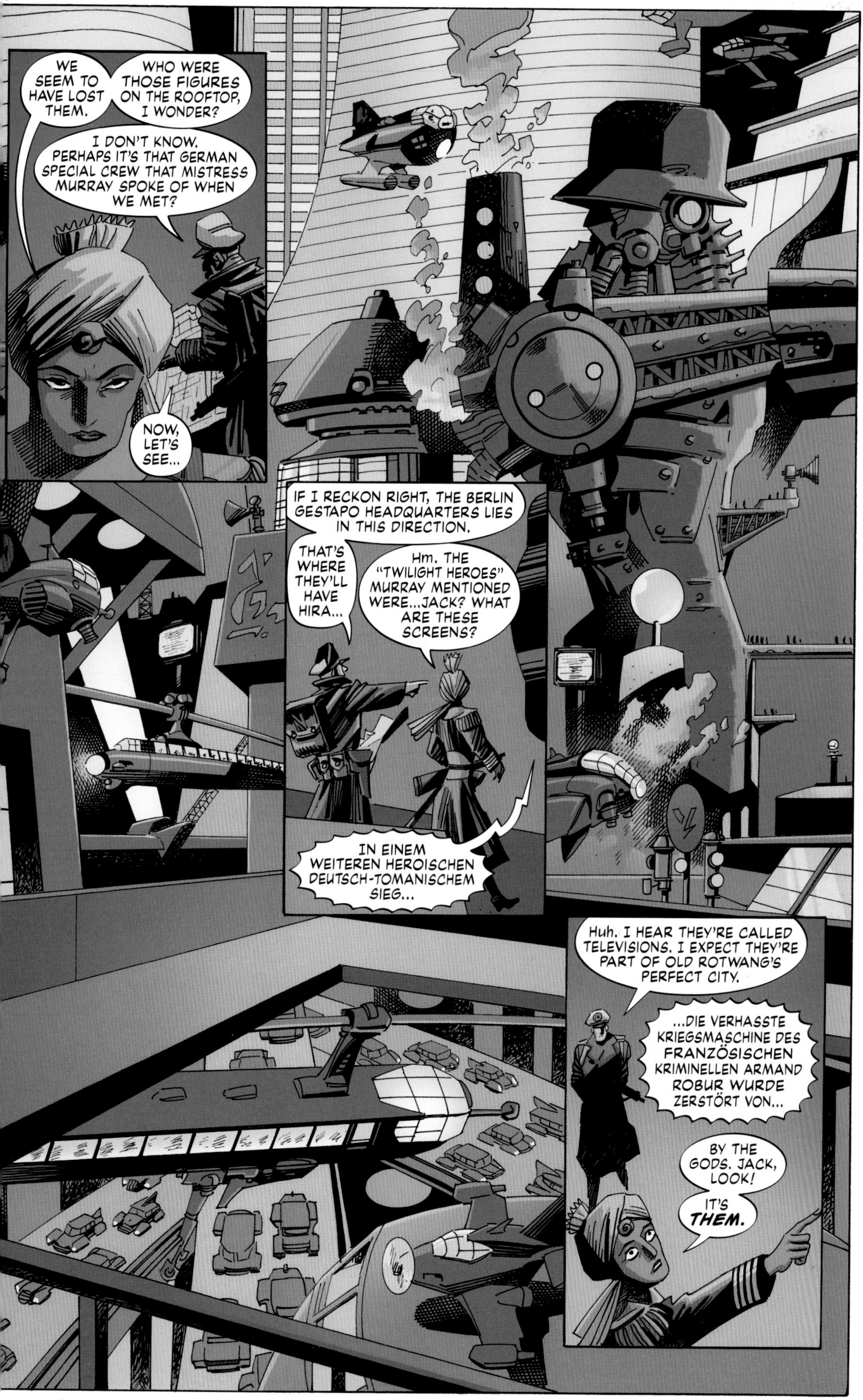

WE SEEM TO HAVE LOST THEM.
WHO WERE THOSE FIGURES ON THE ROOFTOP, I WONDER?
I DON'T KNOW. PERHAPS IT'S THAT GERMAN SPECIAL CREW THAT MISTRESS MURRAY SPOKE OF WHEN WE MET?
NOW, LET'S SEE...
IF I RECKON RIGHT, THE BERLIN GESTAPO HEADQUARTERS LIES IN THIS DIRECTION.
THAT'S WHERE THEY'LL HAVE HIRA...
Hm. THE "TWILIGHT HEROES" MURRAY MENTIONED WERE...JACK? WHAT ARE THESE SCREENS?
IN EINEM WEITEREN HEROISCHEN DEUTSCH-TOMANISCHEM SIEG...
Huh. I HEAR THEY'RE CALLED TELEVISIONS. I EXPECT THEY'RE PART OF OLD ROTWANG'S PERFECT CITY.
...DIE VERHASSTE KRIEGSMASCHINE DES FRANZÖSISCHEN KRIMINELLEN ARMAND ROBUR WURDE ZERSTÖRT VON...
BY THE GODS. JACK, LOOK!
IT'S THEM.

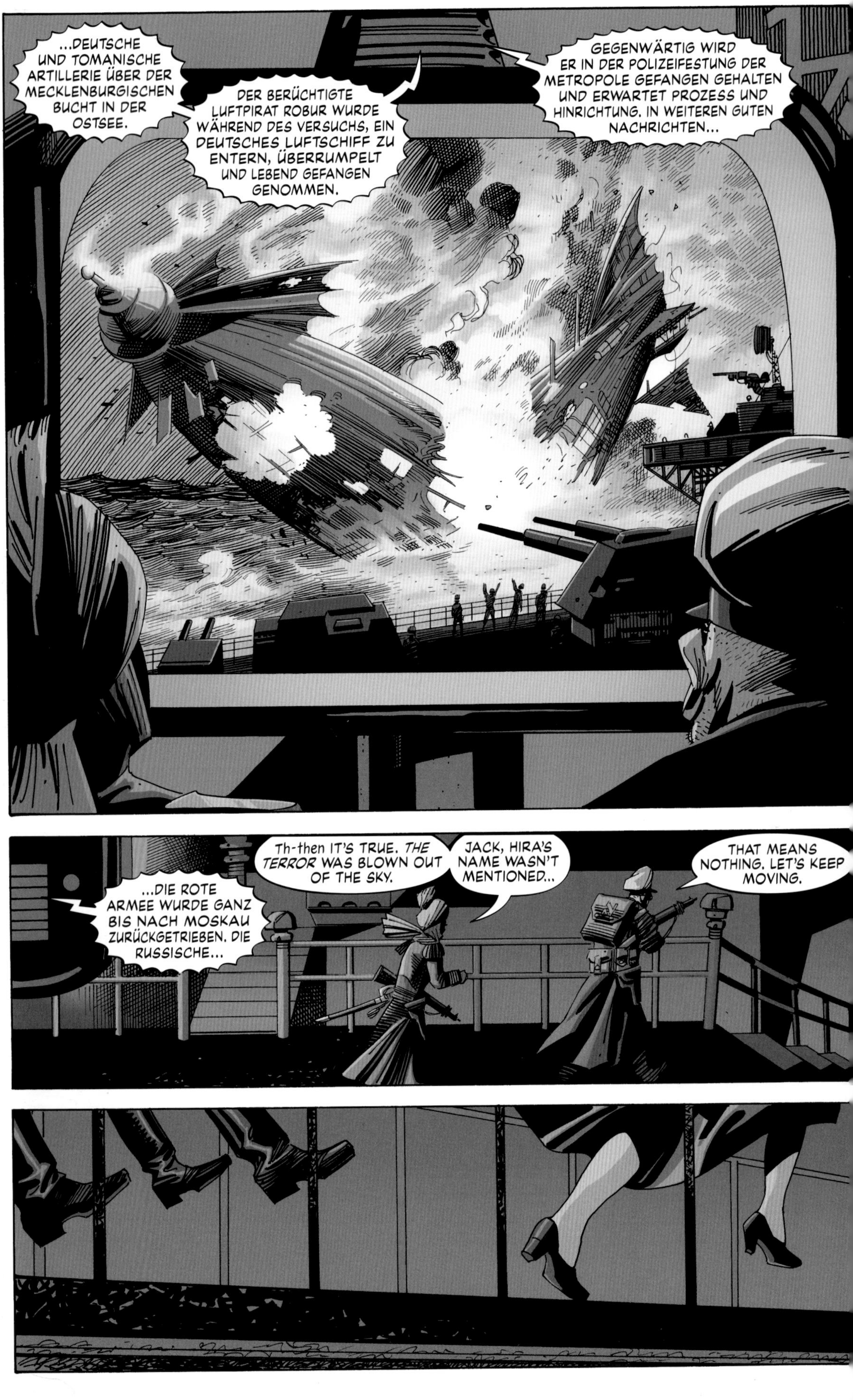
...DEUTSCHE UND TOMANISCHE ARTILLERIE ÜBER DER MECKLENBURGISCHEN BUCHT IN DER OSTSEE.
DER BERÜCHTIGTE LUFTPIRAT ROBUR WURDE WÄHREND DES VERSUCHS, EIN DEUTSCHES LUFTSCHIFF ZU ENTERN, ÜBERRUMPELT UND LEBEND GEFANGEN GENOMMEN.
GEGENWÄRTIG WIRD ER IN DER POLIZEIFESTUNG DER METROPOLE GEFANGEN GEHALTEN UND ERWARTET PROZESS UND HINRICHTUNG. IN WEITEREN GUTEN NACHRICHTEN...
...DIE ROTE ARMEE WURDE GANZ BIS NACH MOSKAU ZURÜCKGETRIEBEN. DIE RUSSISCHE...
Th-then IT'S TRUE. *THE TERROR* WAS BLOWN OUT OF THE SKY.
JACK, HIRA'S NAME WASN'T MENTIONED...
THAT MEANS NOTHING. LET'S KEEP MOVING.

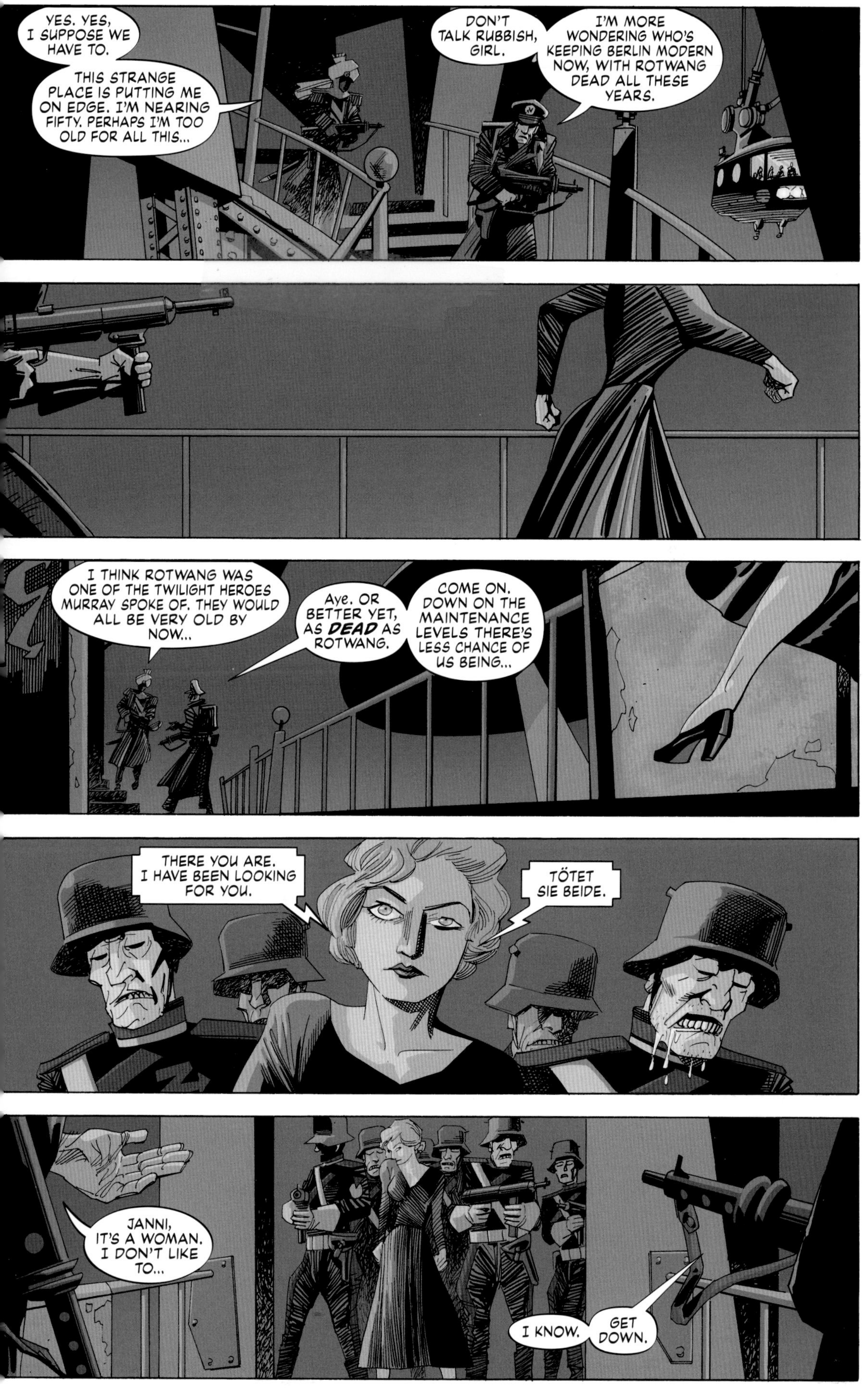
YES. YES, I SUPPOSE WE HAVE TO.
THIS STRANGE PLACE IS PUTTING ME ON EDGE. I'M NEARING FIFTY. PERHAPS I'M TOO OLD FOR ALL THIS...
DON'T TALK RUBBISH, GIRL.
I'M MORE WONDERING WHO'S KEEPING BERLIN MODERN NOW, WITH ROTWANG DEAD ALL THESE YEARS.
I THINK ROTWANG WAS ONE OF THE TWILIGHT HEROES MURRAY SPOKE OF. THEY WOULD ALL BE VERY OLD BY NOW...
Aye. OR BETTER YET, AS *DEAD* AS ROTWANG.
COME ON. DOWN ON THE MAINTENANCE LEVELS THERE'S LESS CHANCE OF US BEING...
THERE YOU ARE. I HAVE BEEN LOOKING FOR YOU.
TÖTET SIE BEIDE.
JANNI, IT'S A WOMAN. I DON'T LIKE TO...
I KNOW.
GET DOWN.

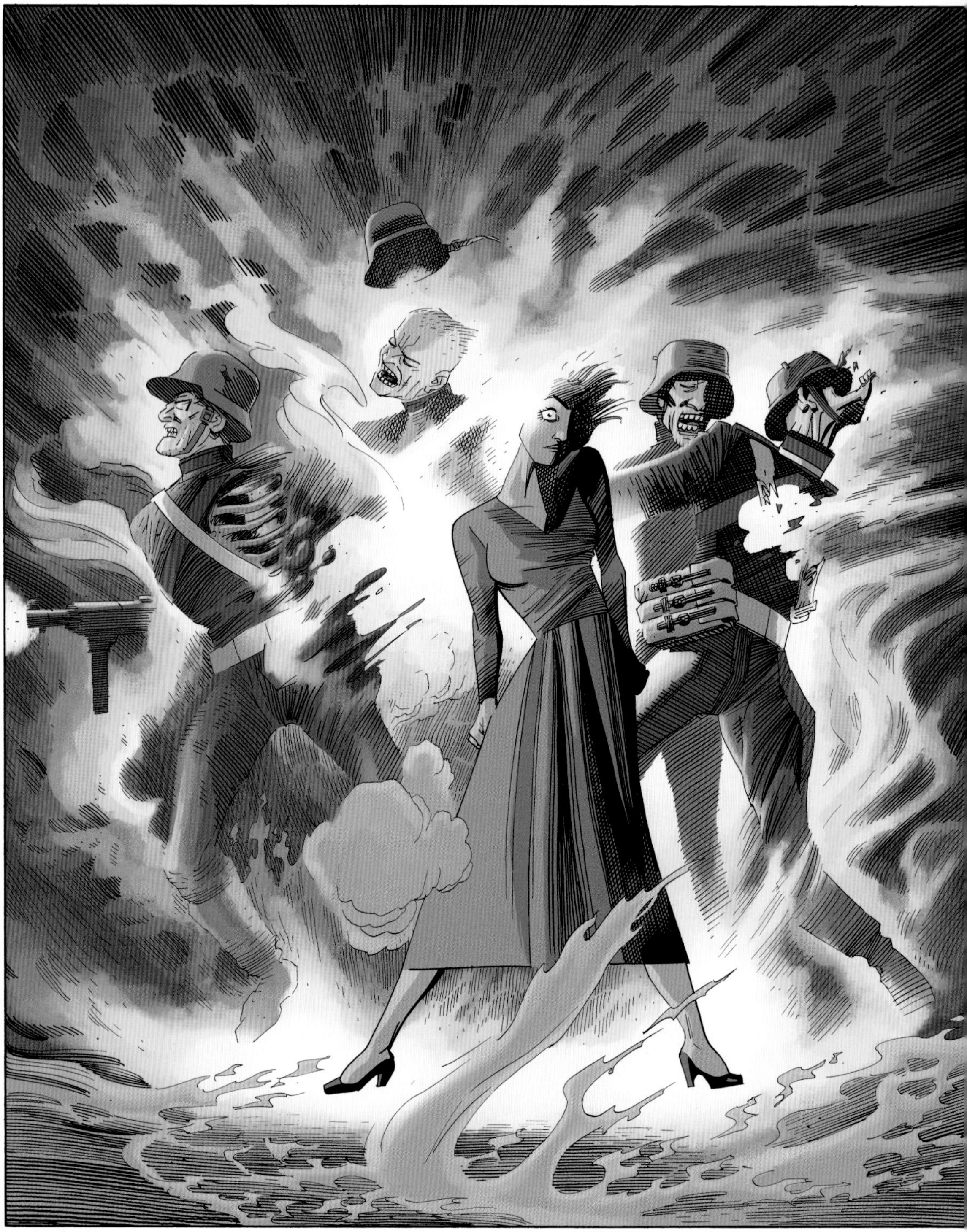

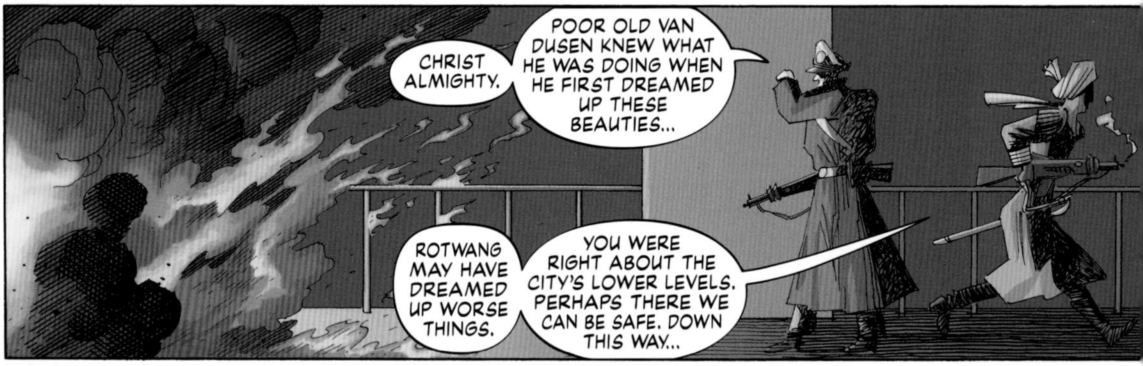

CHRIST ALMIGHTY.
POOR OLD VAN DUSEN KNEW WHAT HE WAS DOING WHEN HE FIRST DREAMED UP THESE BEAUTIES...
ROTWANG MAY HAVE DREAMED UP WORSE THINGS.
YOU WERE RIGHT ABOUT THE CITY'S LOWER LEVELS. PERHAPS THERE WE CAN BE SAFE. DOWN THIS WAY...

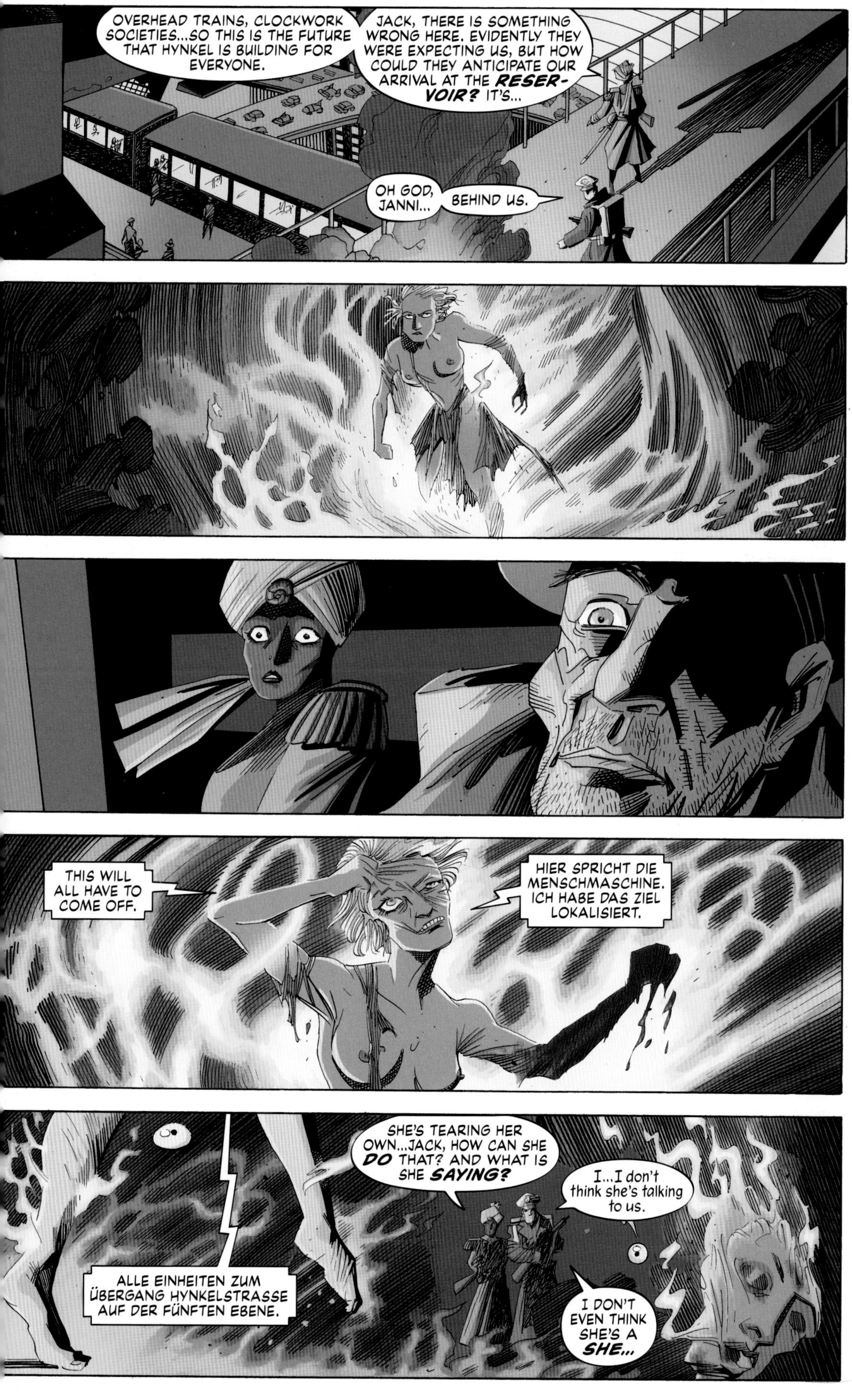

OVERHEAD TRAINS, CLOCKWORK SOCIETIES...SO THIS IS THE FUTURE THAT HYNKEL IS BUILDING FOR EVERYONE.
JACK, THERE IS SOMETHING WRONG HERE. EVIDENTLY THEY WERE EXPECTING US, BUT HOW COULD THEY ANTICIPATE OUR ARRIVAL AT THE RESERVOIR? IT'S...
OH GOD, JANNI...
BEHIND US.
THIS WILL ALL HAVE TO COME OFF.
HIER SPRICHT DIE MENSCHMASCHINE. ICH HABE DAS ZIEL LOKALISIERT.
SHE'S TEARING HER OWN...JACK, HOW CAN SHE DO THAT? AND WHAT IS SHE SAYING?
I...I don't think she's talking to us.
ALLE EINHEITEN ZUM ÜBERGANG HYNKELSTRASSE AUF DER FÜNFTEN EBENE.
I DON'T EVEN THINK SHE'S A SHE...

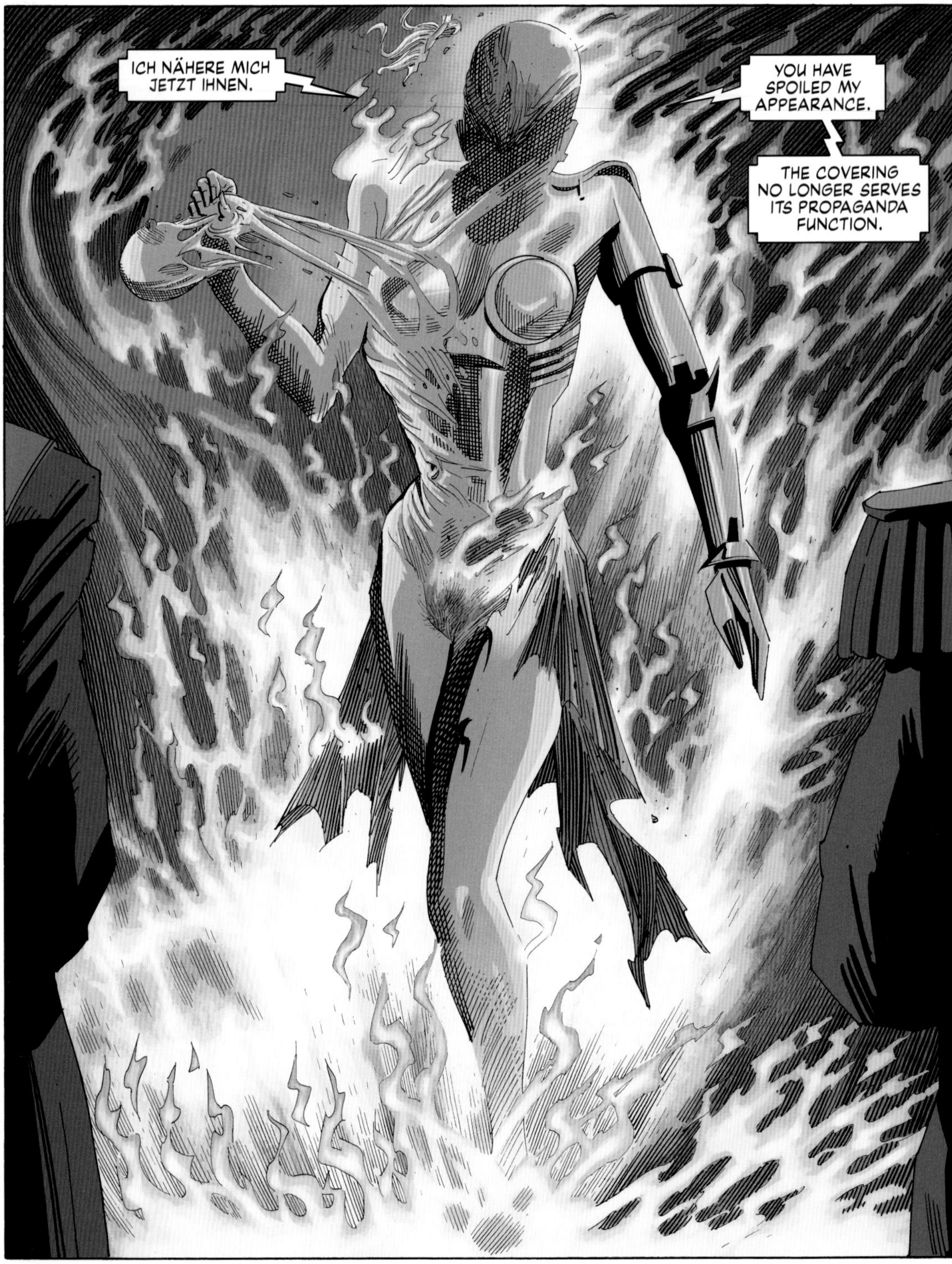
ICH NÄHERE MICH JETZT IHNEN.
YOU HAVE SPOILED MY APPEARANCE.
THE COVERING NO LONGER SERVES ITS PROPAGANDA FUNCTION.

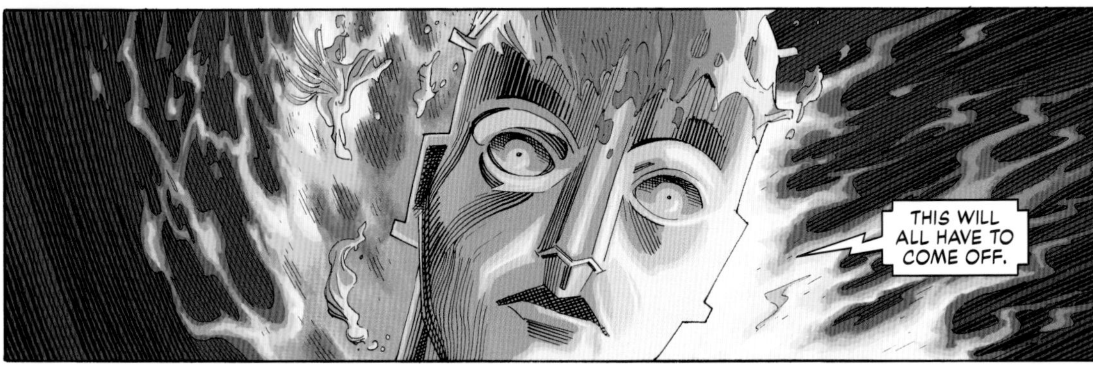
THIS WILL ALL HAVE TO COME OFF.

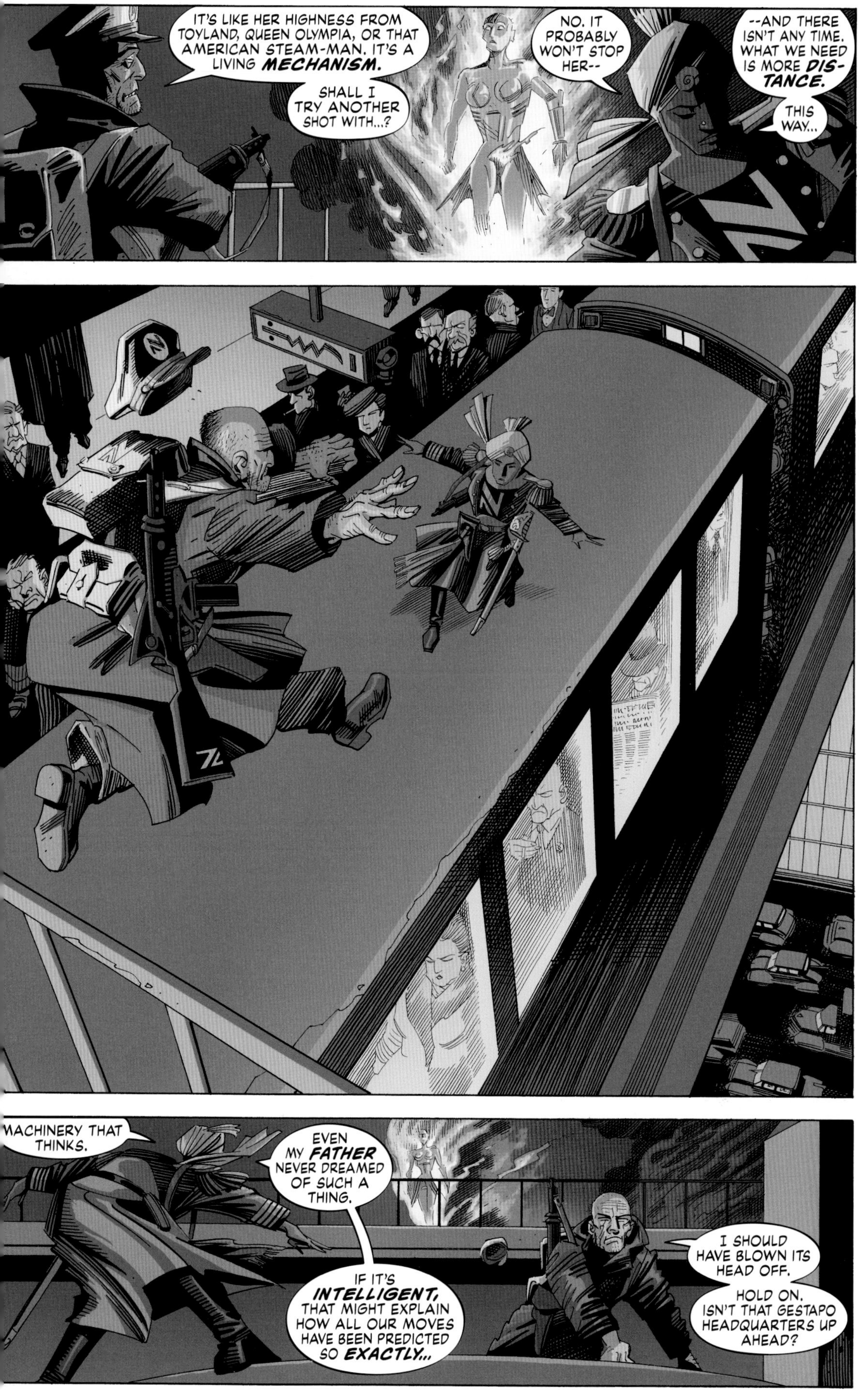
IT'S LIKE HER HIGHNESS FROM TOYLAND, QUEEN OLYMPIA, OR THAT AMERICAN STEAM-MAN. IT'S A LIVING MECHANISM.
SHALL I TRY ANOTHER SHOT WITH...?
NO. IT PROBABLY WON'T STOP HER--
--AND THERE ISN'T ANY TIME. WHAT WE NEED IS MORE DISTANCE.
THIS WAY...
MACHINERY THAT THINKS.
EVEN MY FATHER NEVER DREAMED OF SUCH A THING.
IF IT'S INTELLIGENT, THAT MIGHT EXPLAIN HOW ALL OUR MOVES HAVE BEEN PREDICTED SO EXACTLY...
I SHOULD HAVE BLOWN ITS HEAD OFF.
HOLD ON. ISN'T THAT GESTAPO HEADQUARTERS UP AHEAD?

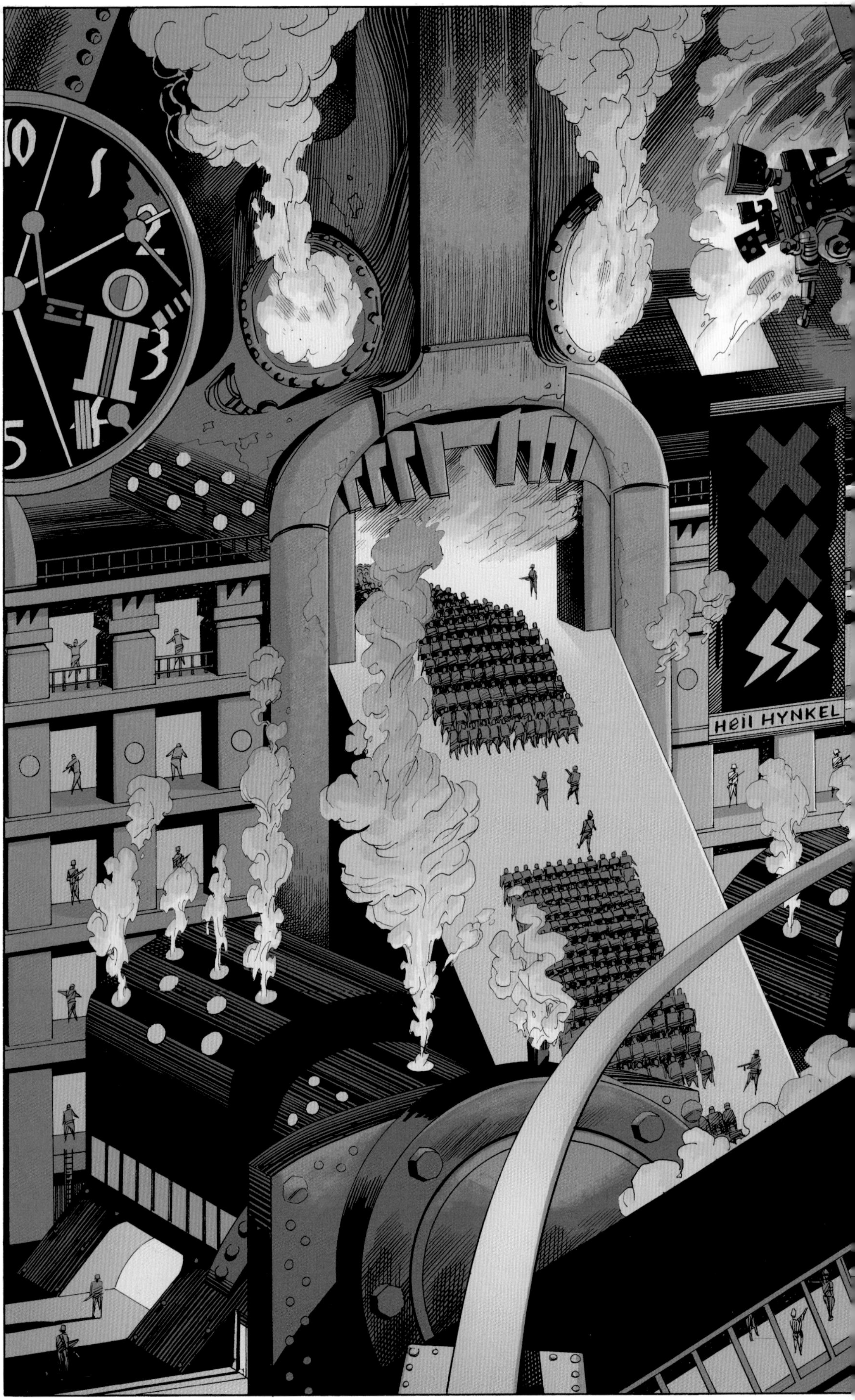
Heil HYNKEL

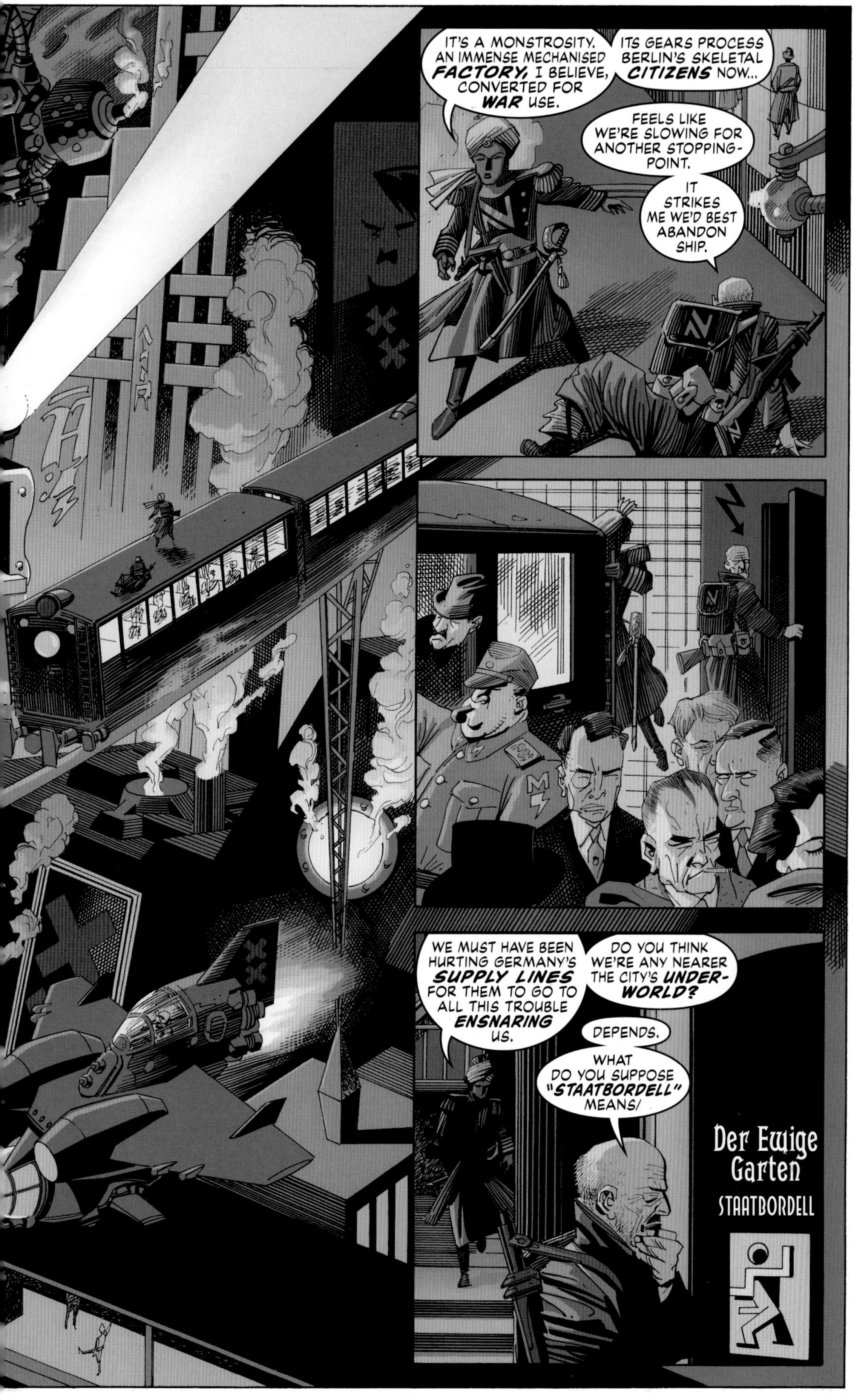

IT'S A MONSTROSITY. AN IMMENSE MECHANISED FACTORY, I BELIEVE, CONVERTED FOR WAR USE.
ITS GEARS PROCESS BERLIN'S SKELETAL CITIZENS NOW...
FEELS LIKE WE'RE SLOWING FOR ANOTHER STOPPING-POINT.
IT STRIKES ME WE'D BEST ABANDON SHIP.
WE MUST HAVE BEEN HURTING GERMANY'S SUPPLY LINES FOR THEM TO GO TO ALL THIS TROUBLE ENSNARING US.
DO YOU THINK WE'RE ANY NEARER THE CITY'S UNDER-WORLD?
DEPENDS.
WHAT DO YOU SUPPOSE "STAATBORDELL" MEANS/
Der Ewige Garten
STAATBORDELL

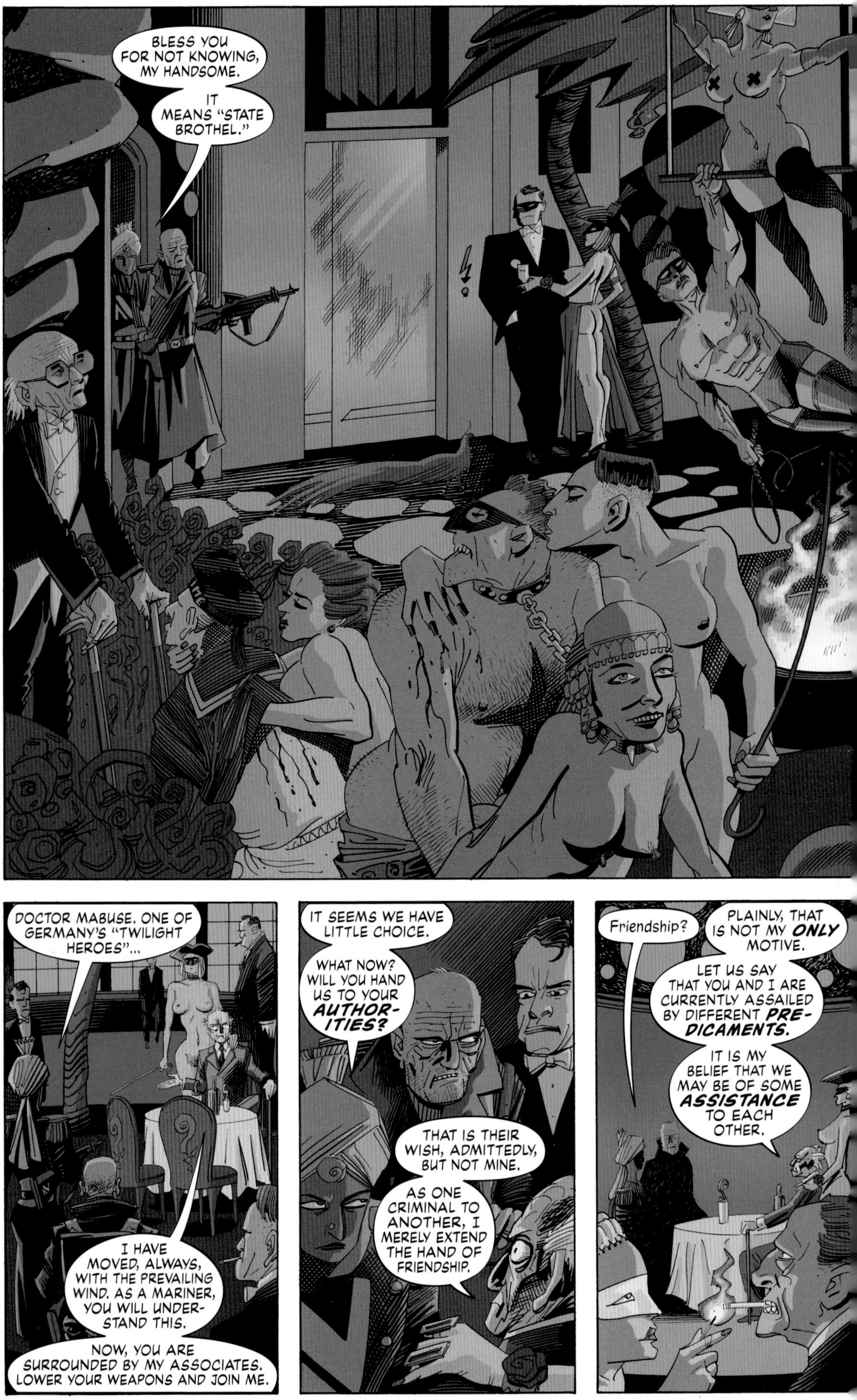
BLESS YOU FOR NOT KNOWING, MY HANDSOME.
IT MEANS "STATE BROTHEL."
DOCTOR MABUSE. ONE OF GERMANY'S "TWILIGHT HEROES"...
I HAVE MOVED, ALWAYS, WITH THE PREVAILING WIND. AS A MARINER, YOU WILL UNDERSTAND THIS.
NOW, YOU ARE SURROUNDED BY MY ASSOCIATES. LOWER YOUR WEAPONS AND JOIN ME.
IT SEEMS WE HAVE LITTLE CHOICE.
WHAT NOW? WILL YOU HAND US TO YOUR AUTHORITIES?
THAT IS THEIR WISH, ADMITTEDLY, BUT NOT MINE.
AS ONE CRIMINAL TO ANOTHER, I MERELY EXTEND THE HAND OF FRIENDSHIP.
Friendship?
PLAINLY, THAT IS NOT MY ONLY MOTIVE.
LET US SAY THAT YOU AND I ARE CURRENTLY ASSAILED BY DIFFERENT PREDICAMENTS.
IT IS MY BELIEF THAT WE MAY BE OF SOME ASSISTANCE TO EACH OTHER.

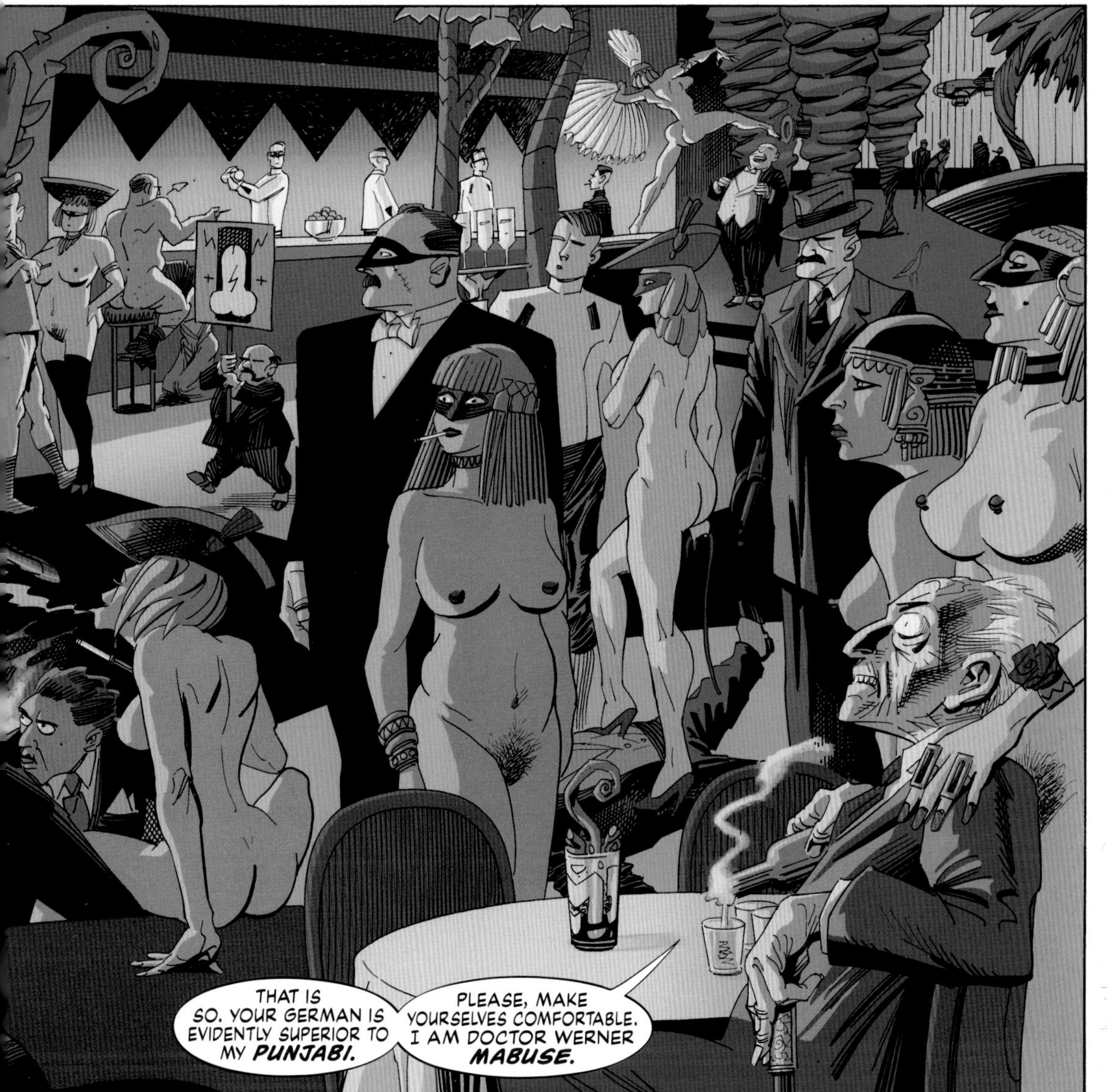
THAT IS SO. YOUR GERMAN IS EVIDENTLY SUPERIOR TO MY PUNJABI.
PLEASE, MAKE YOURSELVES COMFORTABLE. I AM DOCTOR WERNER MABUSE.

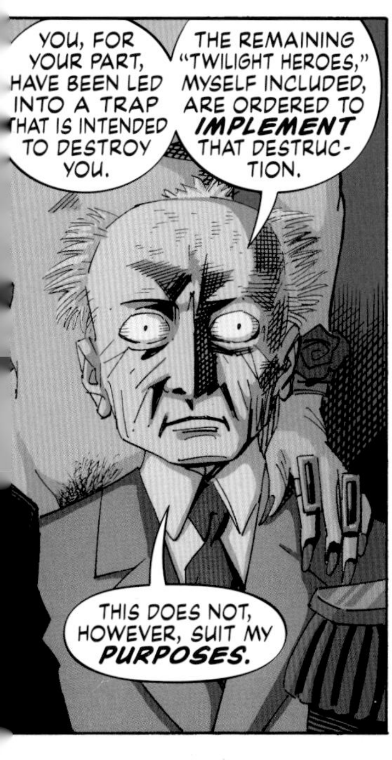
YOU, FOR YOUR PART, HAVE BEEN LED INTO A TRAP THAT IS INTENDED TO DESTROY YOU.
THE REMAINING "TWILIGHT HEROES," MYSELF INCLUDED, ARE ORDERED TO IMPLEMENT THAT DESTRUCTION.
THIS DOES NOT, HOWEVER, SUIT MY PURPOSES.

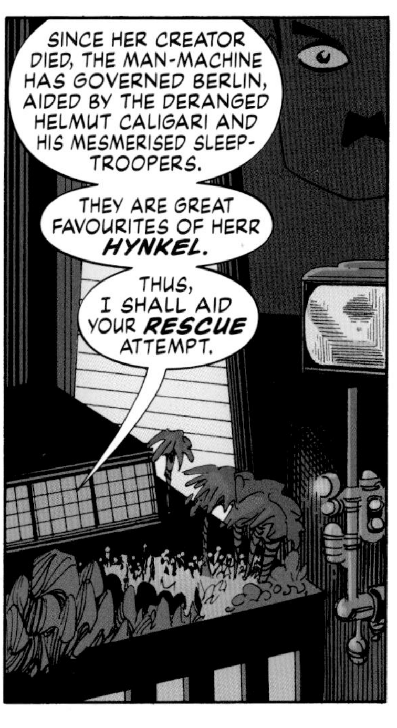
SINCE HER CREATOR DIED, THE MAN-MACHINE HAS GOVERNED BERLIN, AIDED BY THE DERANGED HELMUT CALIGARI AND HIS MESMERISED SLEEP-TROOPERS.
THEY ARE GREAT FAVOURITES OF HERR HYNKEL.
THUS, I SHALL AID YOUR RESCUE ATTEMPT.

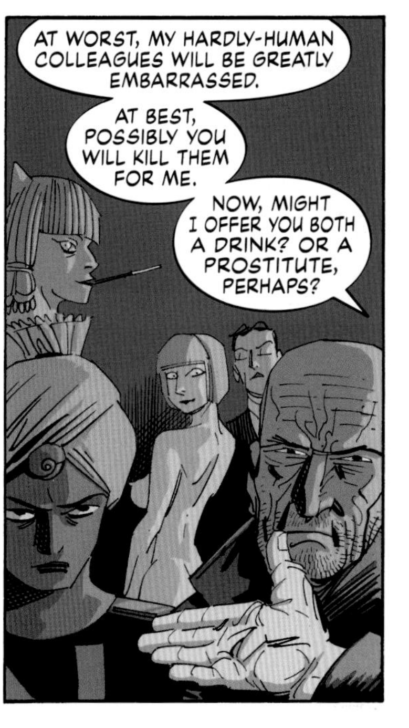
AT WORST, MY HARDLY-HUMAN COLLEAGUES WILL BE GREATLY EMBARRASSED.
AT BEST, POSSIBLY YOU WILL KILL THEM FOR ME.
NOW, MIGHT I OFFER YOU BOTH A DRINK? OR A PROSTITUTE, PERHAPS?

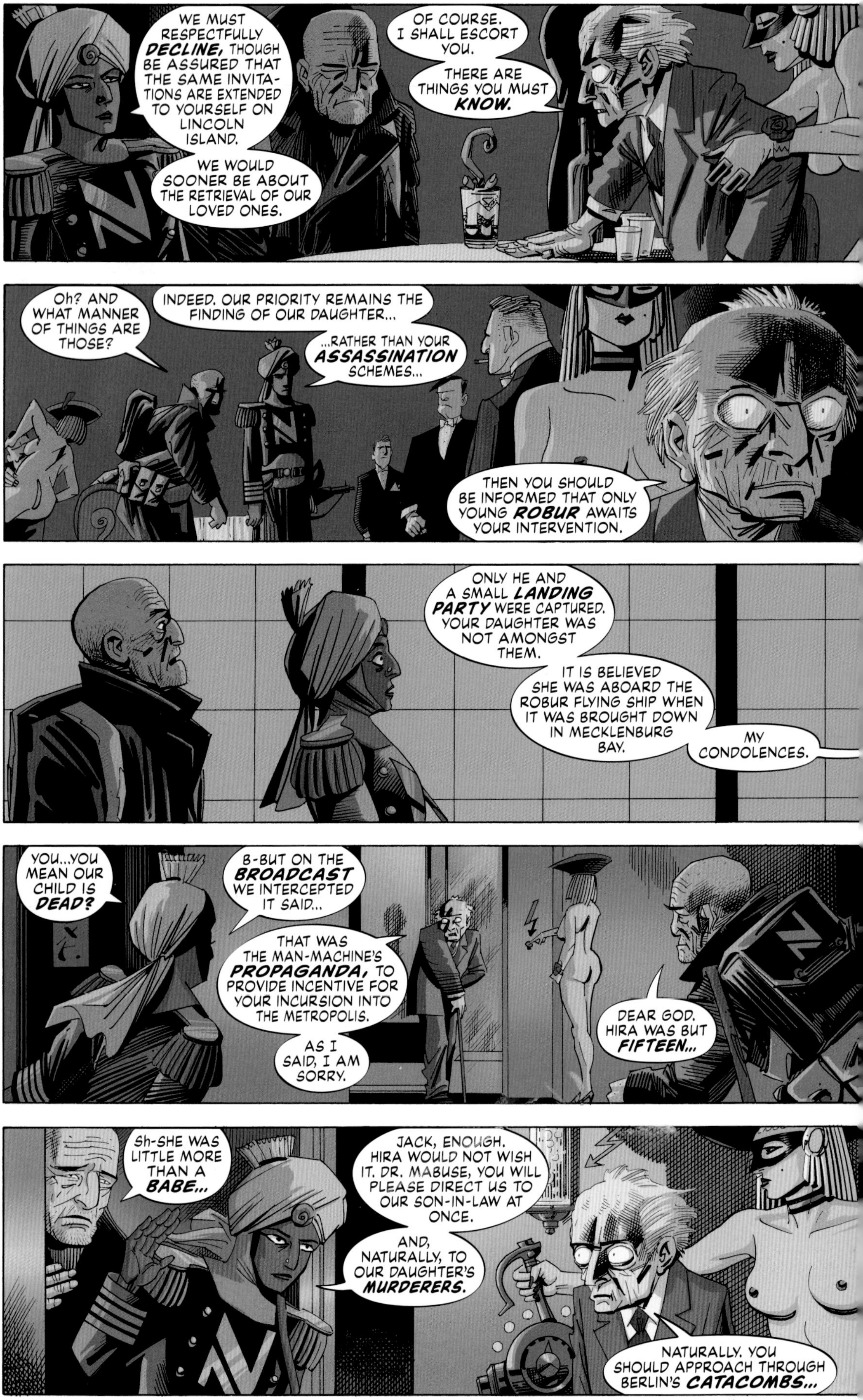

WE MUST RESPECTFULLY DECLINE, THOUGH BE ASSURED THAT THE SAME INVITATIONS ARE EXTENDED TO YOURSELF ON LINCOLN ISLAND.
WE WOULD SOONER BE ABOUT THE RETRIEVAL OF OUR LOVED ONES.
OF COURSE. I SHALL ESCORT YOU.
THERE ARE THINGS YOU MUST KNOW.
Oh? AND WHAT MANNER OF THINGS ARE THOSE?
INDEED. OUR PRIORITY REMAINS THE FINDING OF OUR DAUGHTER...
...RATHER THAN YOUR ASSASSINATION SCHEMES...
THEN YOU SHOULD BE INFORMED THAT ONLY YOUNG ROBUR AWAITS YOUR INTERVENTION.
ONLY HE AND A SMALL LANDING PARTY WERE CAPTURED. YOUR DAUGHTER WAS NOT AMONGST THEM.
IT IS BELIEVED SHE WAS ABOARD THE ROBUR FLYING SHIP WHEN IT WAS BROUGHT DOWN IN MECKLENBURG BAY.
MY CONDOLENCES.
YOU...YOU MEAN OUR CHILD IS DEAD?
B-BUT ON THE BROADCAST WE INTERCEPTED IT SAID...
THAT WAS THE MAN-MACHINE'S PROPAGANDA, TO PROVIDE INCENTIVE FOR YOUR INCURSION INTO THE METROPOLIS.
AS I SAID, I AM SORRY.
DEAR GOD. HIRA WAS BUT FIFTEEN...
Sh-SHE WAS LITTLE MORE THAN A BABE...
JACK, ENOUGH. HIRA WOULD NOT WISH IT. DR. MABUSE, YOU WILL PLEASE DIRECT US TO OUR SON-IN-LAW AT ONCE.
AND, NATURALLY, TO OUR DAUGHTER'S MURDERERS.
NATURALLY. YOU SHOULD APPROACH THROUGH BERLIN'S CATACOMBS...

YOUR RELATIVE IS INCARCERATED INSIDE THE FORMER *MOLOCH MACHINE.* THE SHE-AUTOMATON PREDICTED YOUR ASSAULT WOULD BE A *FRONTAL* ONE.

HOWEVER, AN UNGUARDED REAR WALL I KNOW OF MIGHT BE BREACHED BY YOUR NEW HARPOON-WEAPONS.

ROTWANG'S MANIKIN HAS NOT ANTICIPATED *THOSE.*

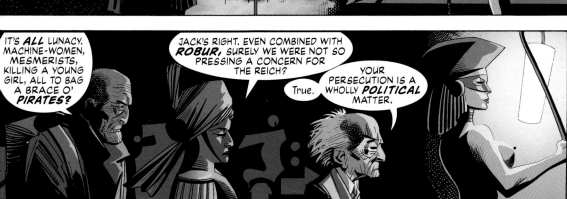

LET'S HOPE NOT. WE CERTAINLY HADN'T ANTICIPATED *HER,* OR THOSE SHUFFLING *SOLDIERS.*

THE MAN-MACHINE IS *RESILIENT,* BUT PROBABLY VULNERABLE TO SUSTAINED *FIRE-POWER.*

DEVELOPED AFTER THE DEATH OF HIS ORIGINAL SOMNAMBULIST, CALIGARI'S SLEEP-COMMANDOS ARE MORE *PROBLEMATIC,* BUT WITHOUT HIM, *DIRECTIONLESS.*

IT'S *ALL* LUNACY. MACHINE-WOMEN, MESMERISTS, KILLING A YOUNG GIRL, ALL TO BAG A BRACE O' *PIRATES?*

JACK'S RIGHT. EVEN COMBINED WITH *ROBUR,* SURELY WE WERE NOT SO PRESSING A CONCERN FOR THE REICH?

True.

YOUR PERSECUTION IS A WHOLLY *POLITICAL* MATTER.

How so?

YOU MUST UNDERSTAND THAT *ALONE,* HERR HYNKEL IS A SOLITARY MANIAC INTENT UPON EXTERMINAT-ING JEWS AND BRUNETTES. HE DEPENDS UPON *ALLIANCES.*

THUS HE STRIKES DEALS WITH *MECCANIA,* OR WITH BENZINO NAPALONI OF *BACTERIA.*

CURRENTLY, HE IS SEEKING ALLIES IN *AFRICA.*

HIS CAMPAIGN THERE CANNOT SUCCEED WITHOUT THE COOPERATION OF A LOCAL *MONARCH.*

REGRETTABLY, IT SEEMS THIS POTENTATE HAS MADE YOUR EXECUTION A CONDITION OF THEIR UNION WITH GERMANY-TOMANIA. I KNOW NOTHING MORE.

HOWEVER, I DO POSSESS A *PHOTOGRAPH* OF THIS PERSON...

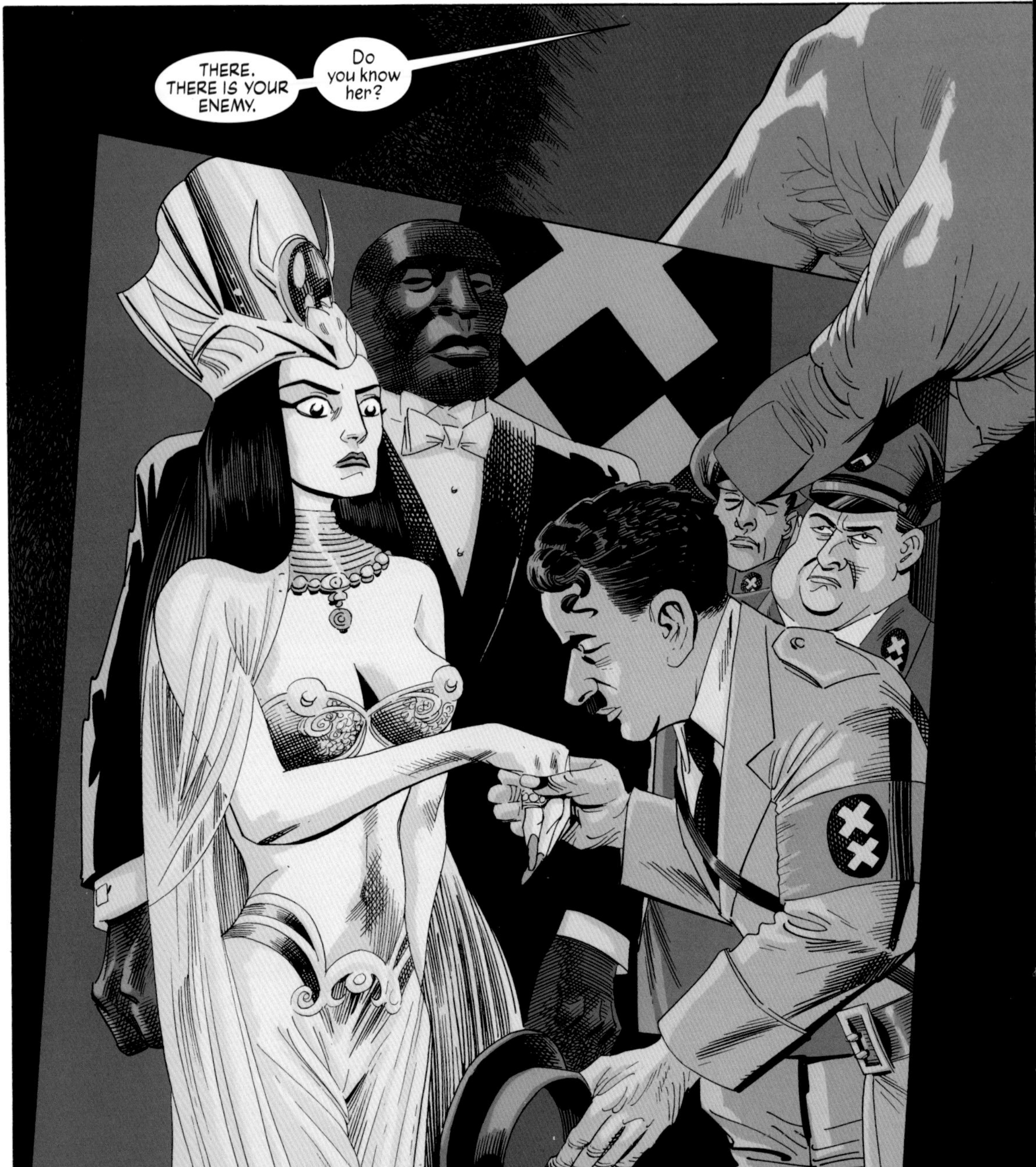
THERE. THERE IS YOUR ENEMY.
Do you know her?

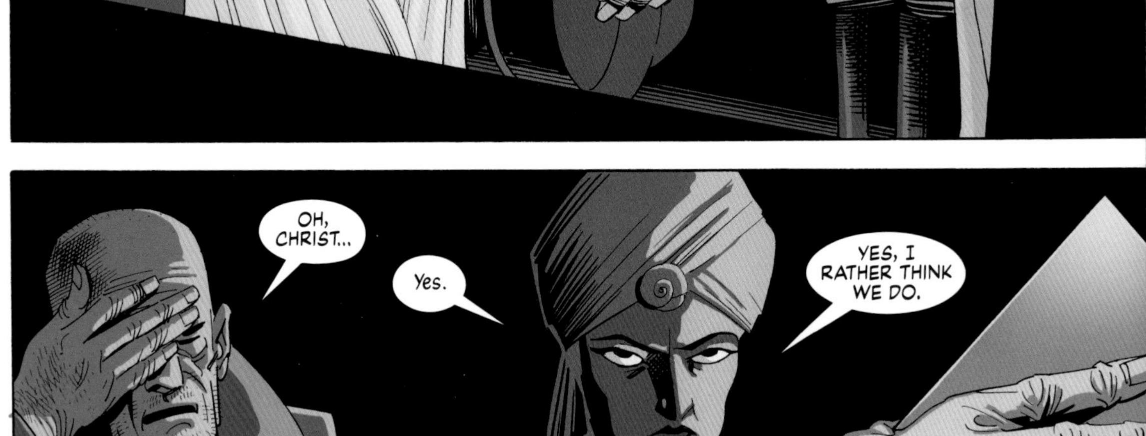
OH, CHRIST...
Yes.
YES, I RATHER THINK WE DO.

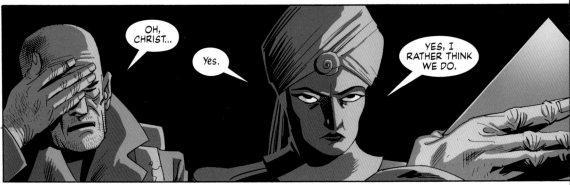

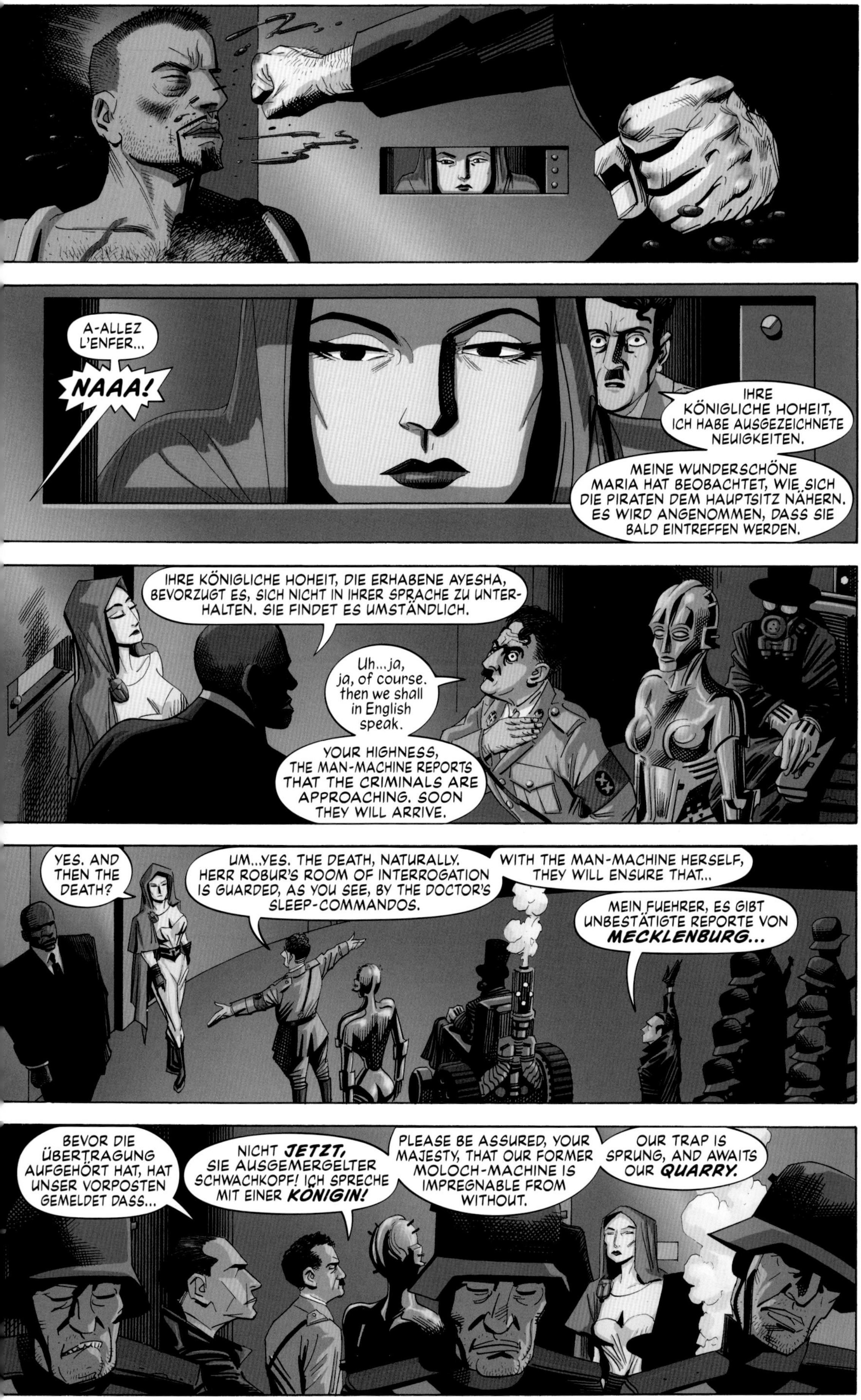
A-ALLEZ L'ENFER...
NAAA!
IHRE KÖNIGLICHE HOHEIT, ICH HABE AUSGEZEICHNETE NEUIGKEITEN.
MEINE WUNDERSCHÖNE MARIA HAT BEOBACHTET, WIE SICH DIE PIRATEN DEM HAUPTSITZ NÄHERN. ES WIRD ANGENOMMEN, DASS SIE BALD EINTREFFEN WERDEN.
IHRE KÖNIGLICHE HOHEIT, DIE ERHABENE AYESHA, BEVORZUGT ES, SICH NICHT IN IHRER SPRACHE ZU UNTERHALTEN. SIE FINDET ES UMSTÄNDLICH.
Uh...ja, ja, of course. then we shall in English speak.
YOUR HIGHNESS, THE MAN-MACHINE REPORTS THAT THE CRIMINALS ARE APPROACHING. SOON THEY WILL ARRIVE.
YES. AND THEN THE DEATH?
UM...YES. THE DEATH, NATURALLY. HERR ROBUR'S ROOM OF INTERROGATION IS GUARDED, AS YOU SEE, BY THE DOCTOR'S SLEEP-COMMANDOS.
WITH THE MAN-MACHINE HERSELF, THEY WILL ENSURE THAT...
MEIN FUEHRER, ES GIBT UNBESTÄTIGTE REPORTE VON MECKLENBURG...
BEVOR DIE ÜBERTRAGUNG AUFGEHÖRT HAT, HAT UNSER VORPOSTEN GEMELDET DASS...
NICHT JETZT, SIE AUSGEMERGELTER SCHWACHKOPF! ICH SPRECHE MIT EINER KÖNIGIN!
PLEASE BE ASSURED, YOUR MAJESTY, THAT OUR FORMER MOLOCH-MACHINE IS IMPREGNABLE FROM WITHOUT.
OUR TRAP IS SPRUNG, AND AWAITS OUR QUARRY.

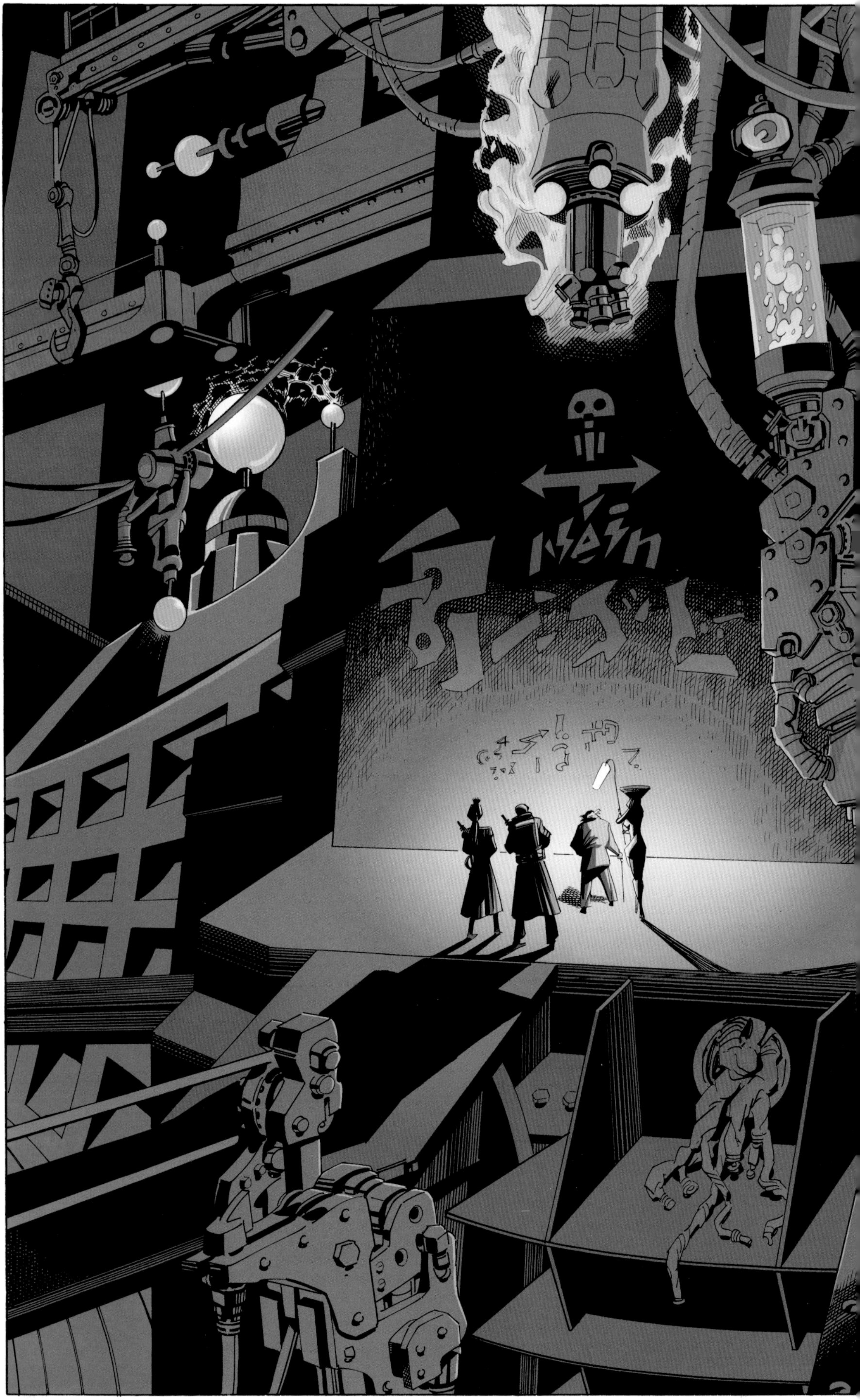

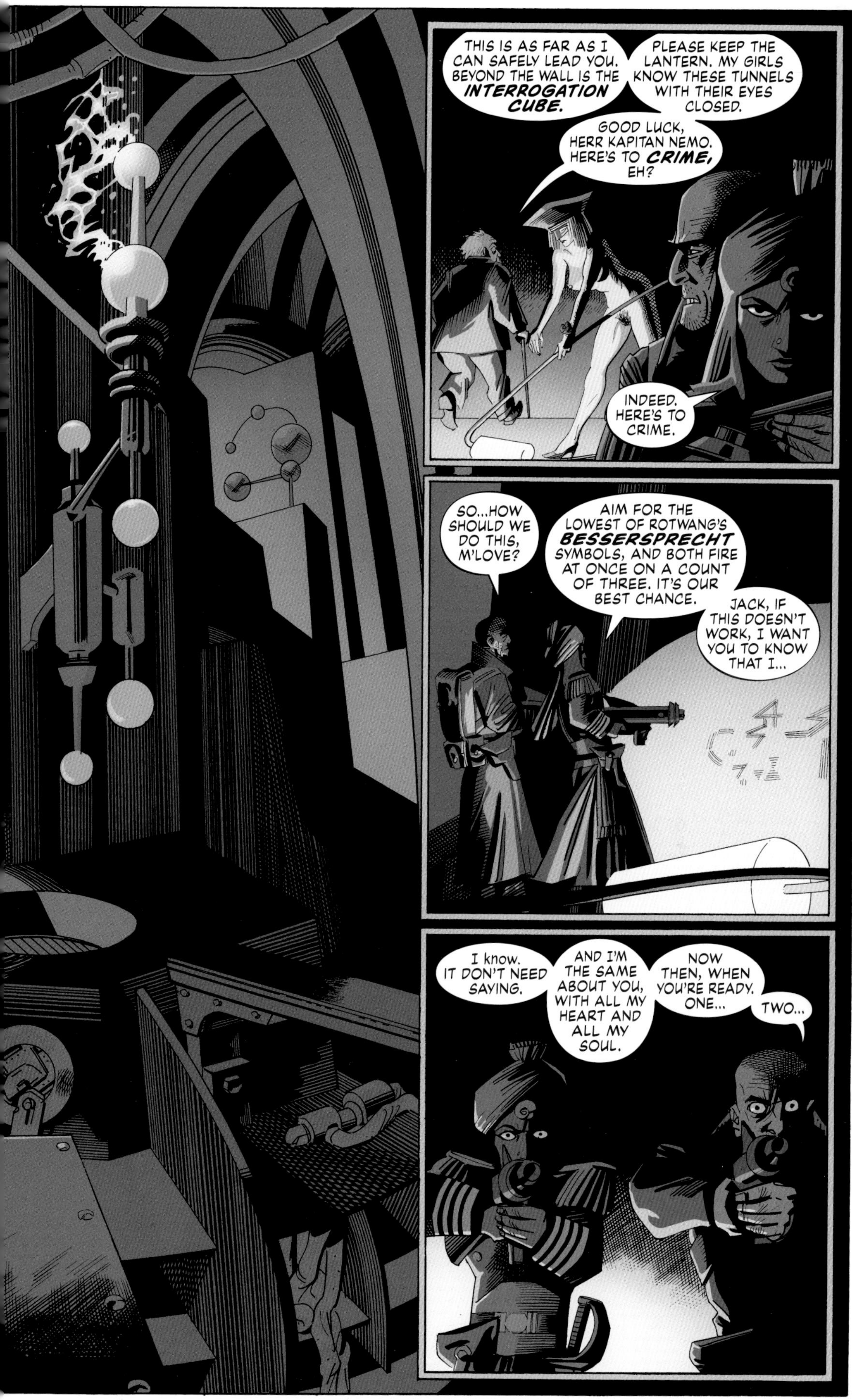
THIS IS AS FAR AS I CAN SAFELY LEAD YOU. BEYOND THE WALL IS THE INTERROGATION CUBE.
PLEASE KEEP THE LANTERN. MY GIRLS KNOW THESE TUNNELS WITH THEIR EYES CLOSED.
GOOD LUCK, HERR KAPITAN NEMO. HERE'S TO CRIME, EH?
INDEED. HERE'S TO CRIME.
SO...HOW SHOULD WE DO THIS, M'LOVE?
AIM FOR THE LOWEST OF ROTWANG'S BESSERSPRECHT SYMBOLS, AND BOTH FIRE AT ONCE ON A COUNT OF THREE. IT'S OUR BEST CHANCE.
JACK, IF THIS DOESN'T WORK, I WANT YOU TO KNOW THAT I...
I know. IT DON'T NEED SAYING.
AND I'M THE SAME ABOUT YOU, WITH ALL MY HEART AND ALL MY SOUL.
NOW THEN, WHEN YOU'RE READY. ONE...
TWO...

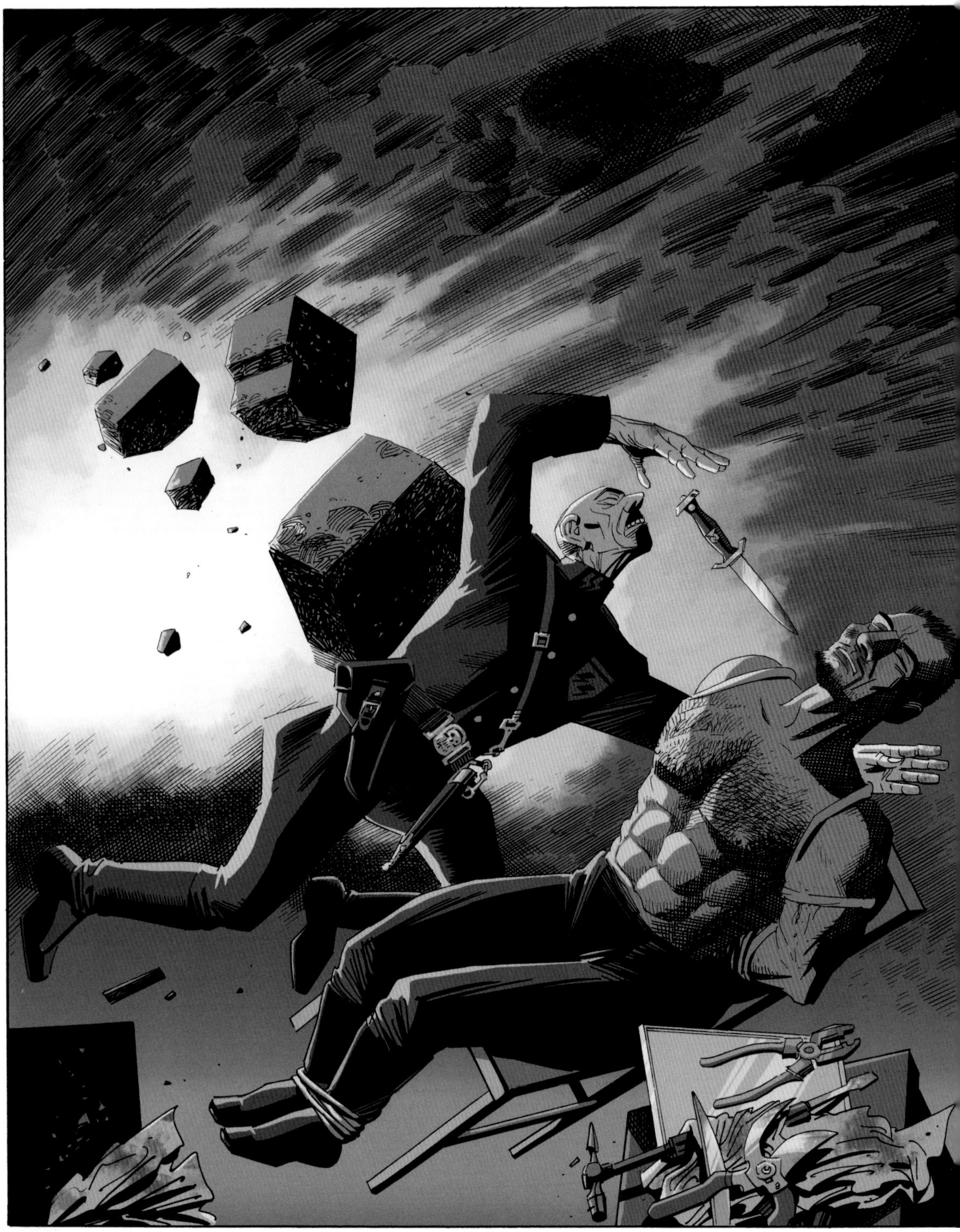

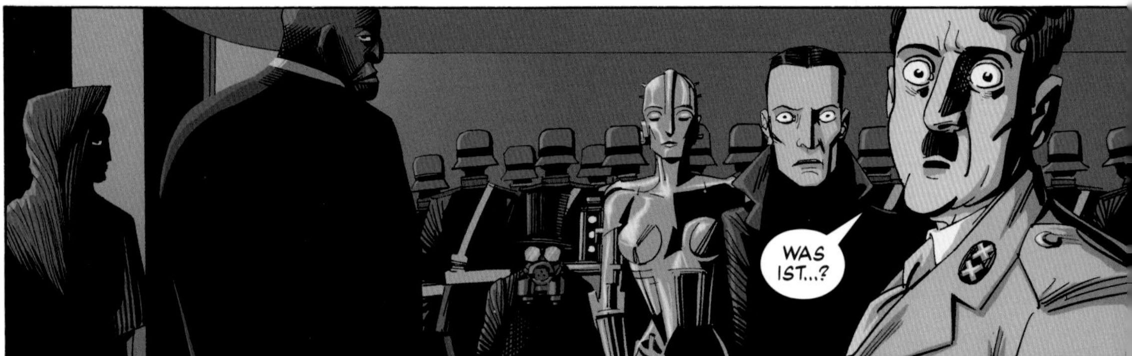
WAS IST...?

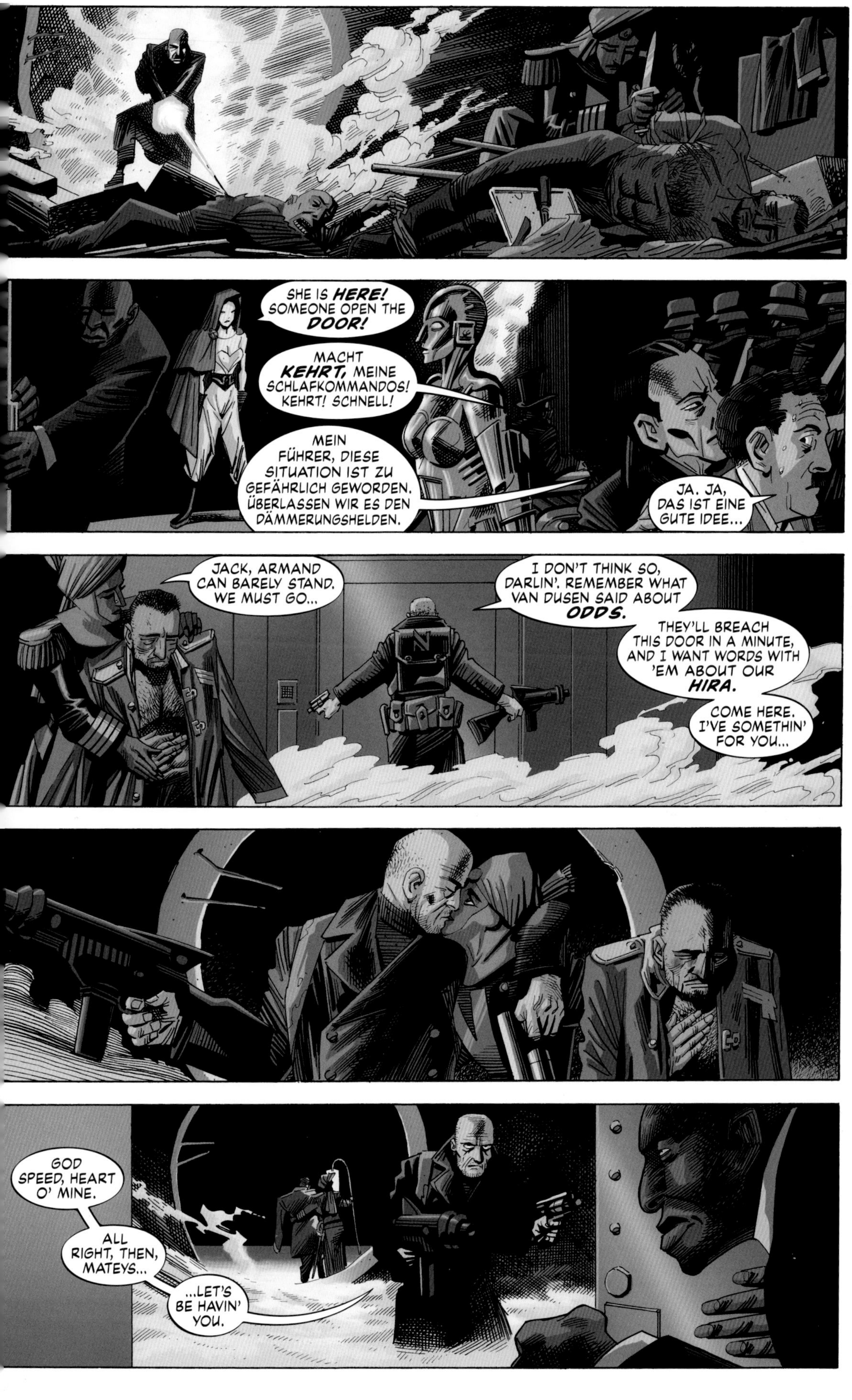

SHE IS HERE! SOMEONE OPEN THE DOOR!
MACHT KEHRT, MEINE SCHLAFKOMMANDOS! KEHRT! SCHNELL!
MEIN FÜHRER, DIESE SITUATION IST ZU GEFÄHRLICH GEWORDEN. ÜBERLASSEN WIR ES DEN DÄMMERUNGSHELDEN.
JA. JA, DAS IST EINE GUTE IDEE...
JACK, ARMAND CAN BARELY STAND. WE MUST GO...
I DON'T THINK SO, DARLIN'. REMEMBER WHAT VAN DUSEN SAID ABOUT ODDS.
THEY'LL BREACH THIS DOOR IN A MINUTE, AND I WANT WORDS WITH 'EM ABOUT OUR HIRA.
COME HERE. I'VE SOMETHIN' FOR YOU...
GOD SPEED, HEART O' MINE.
ALL RIGHT, THEN, MATEYS...
...LET'S BE HAVIN' YOU.

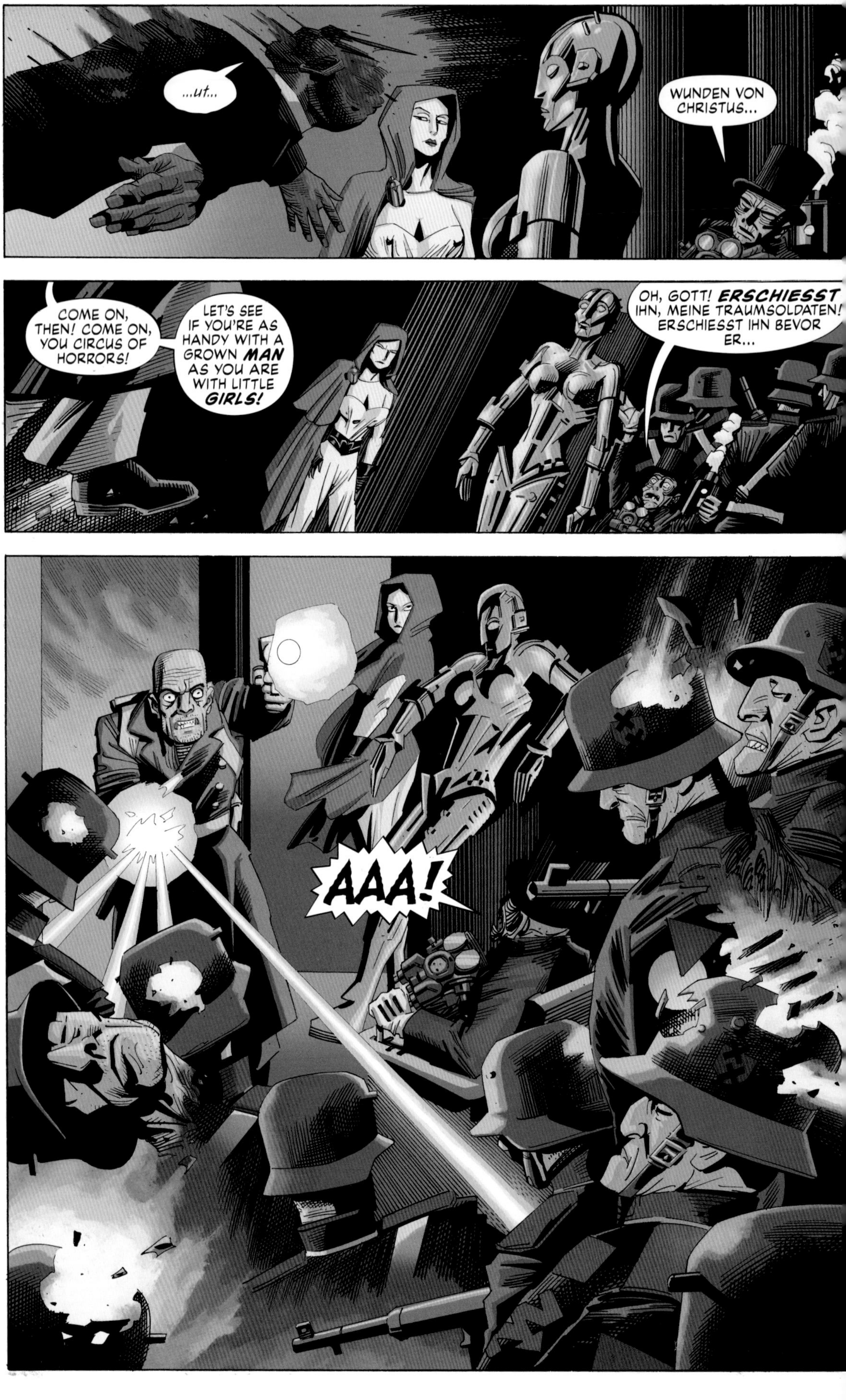
...ut...
WUNDEN VON CHRISTUS...
COME ON, THEN! COME ON, YOU CIRCUS OF HORRORS!
LET'S SEE IF YOU'RE AS HANDY WITH A GROWN MAN AS YOU ARE WITH LITTLE GIRLS!
OH, GOTT! ERSCHIESST IHN, MEINE TRAUMSOLDATEN! ERSCHIESST IHN BEVOR ER...
AAA!

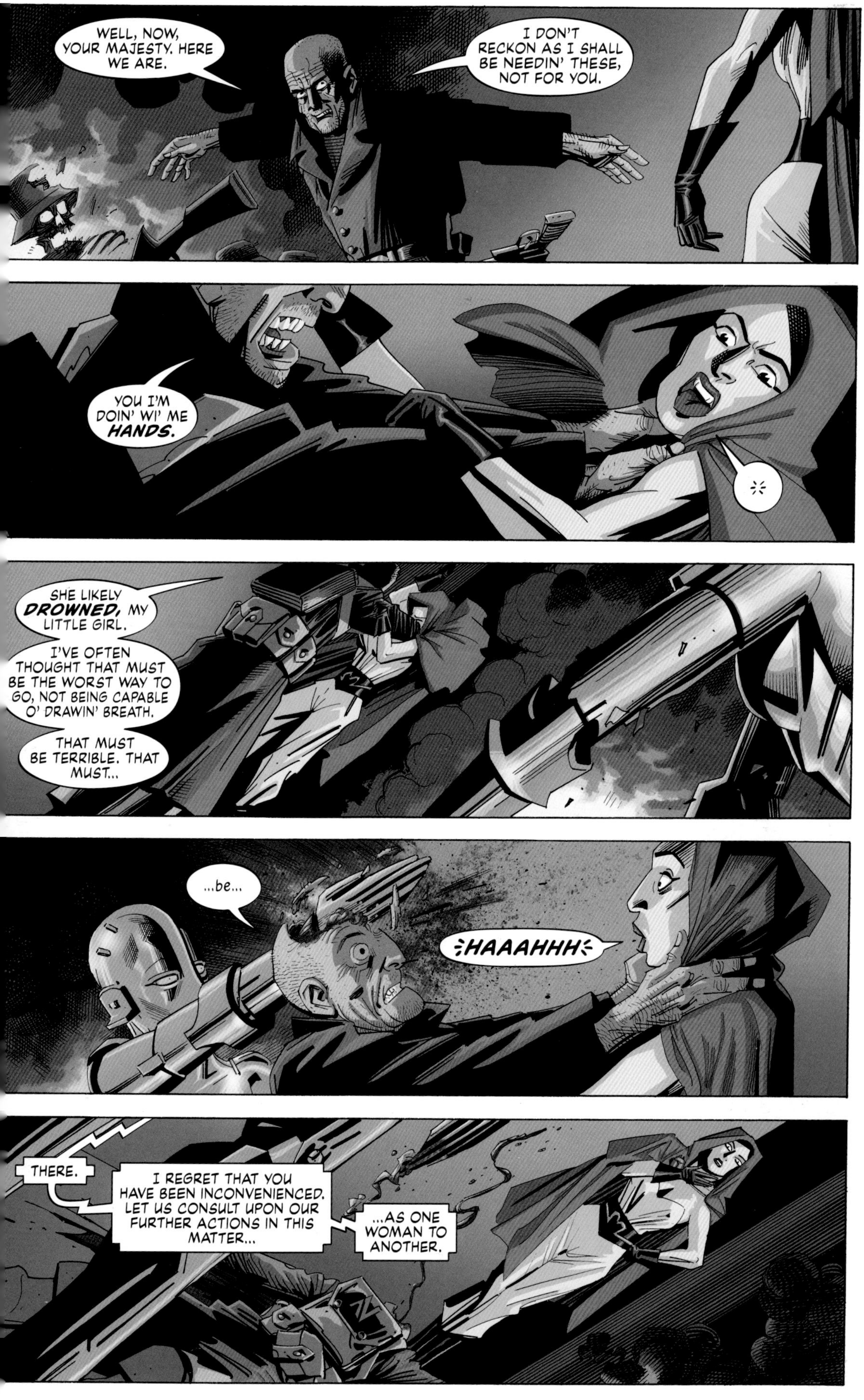
WELL, NOW, YOUR MAJESTY. HERE WE ARE.
I DON'T RECKON AS I SHALL BE NEEDIN' THESE, NOT FOR YOU.
YOU I'M DOIN' WI' ME HANDS.
SHE LIKELY DROWNED, MY LITTLE GIRL.
I'VE OFTEN THOUGHT THAT MUST BE THE WORST WAY TO GO, NOT BEING CAPABLE O' DRAWIN' BREATH.
THAT MUST BE TERRIBLE. THAT MUST...
...be...
HAAAHHH
THERE.
I REGRET THAT YOU HAVE BEEN INCONVENIENCED. LET US CONSULT UPON OUR FURTHER ACTIONS IN THIS MATTER...
...AS ONE WOMAN TO ANOTHER.

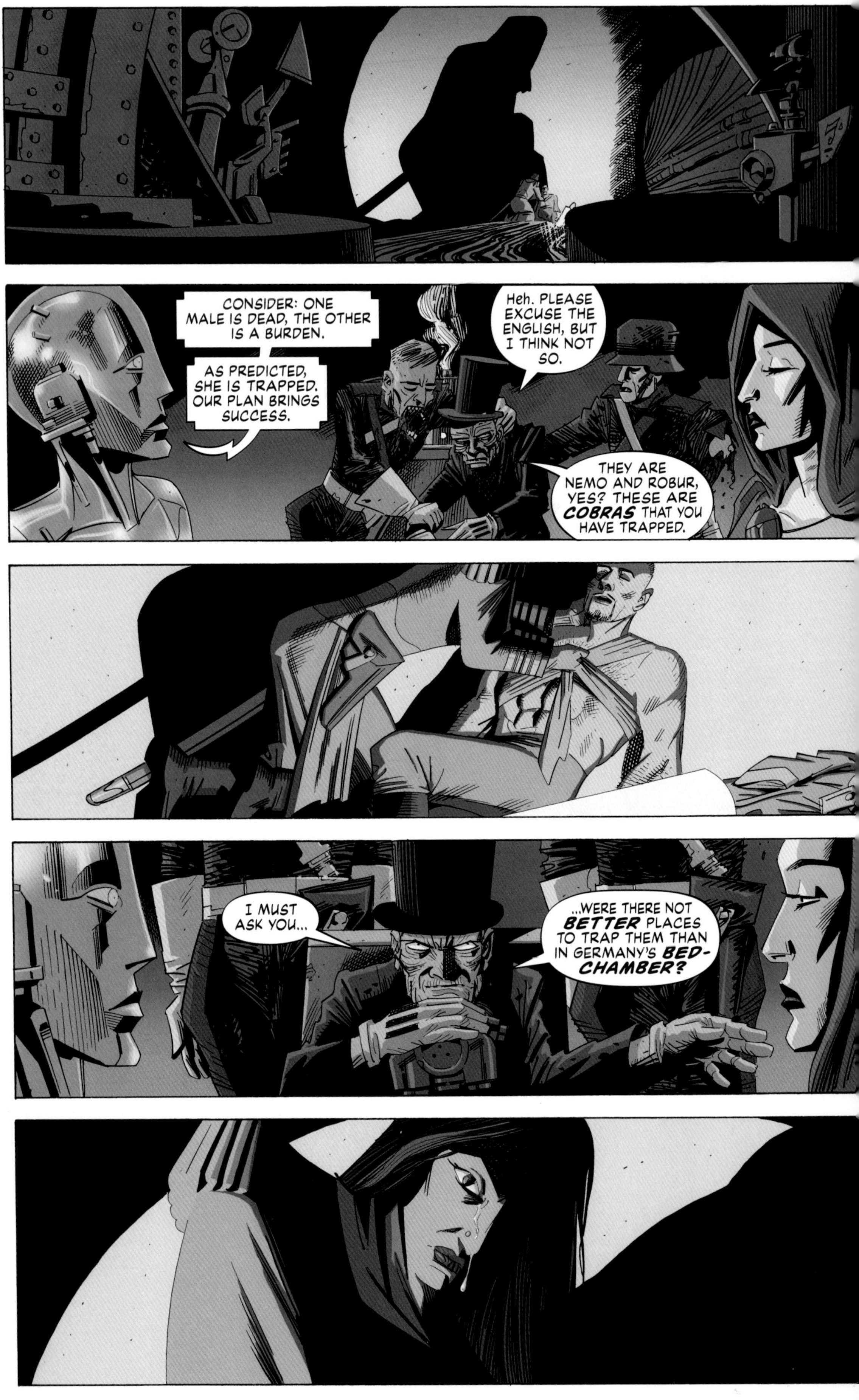
CONSIDER: ONE MALE IS DEAD, THE OTHER IS A BURDEN.
AS PREDICTED, SHE IS TRAPPED. OUR PLAN BRINGS SUCCESS.
Heh. PLEASE EXCUSE THE ENGLISH, BUT I THINK NOT SO.
THEY ARE NEMO AND ROBUR, YES? THESE ARE COBRAS THAT YOU HAVE TRAPPED.
I MUST ASK YOU...
...WERE THERE NOT BETTER PLACES TO TRAP THEM THAN IN GERMANY'S BED-CHAMBER?

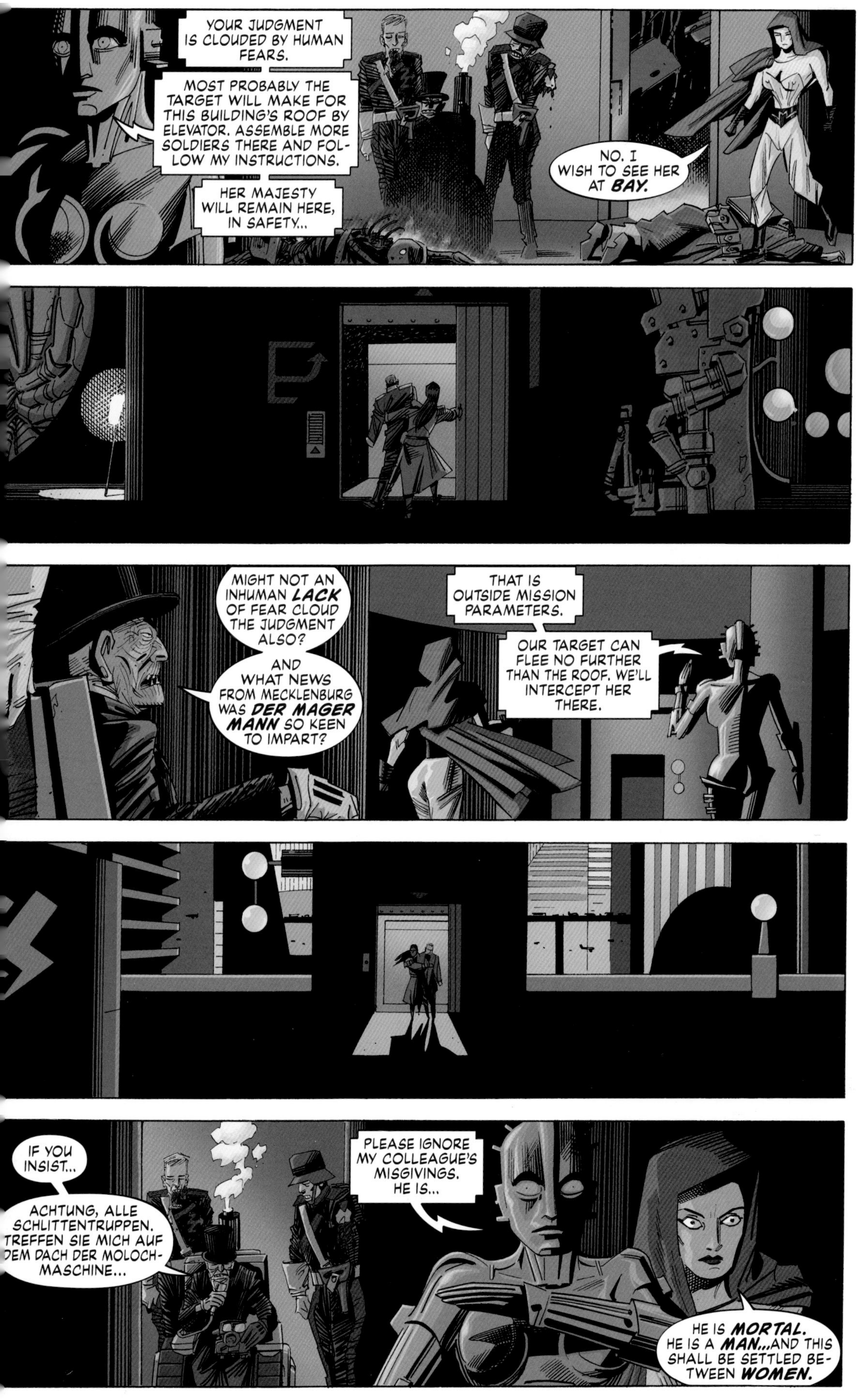
YOUR JUDGMENT IS CLOUDED BY HUMAN FEARS.
MOST PROBABLY THE TARGET WILL MAKE FOR THIS BUILDING'S ROOF BY ELEVATOR. ASSEMBLE MORE SOLDIERS THERE AND FOL-LOW MY INSTRUCTIONS.
HER MAJESTY WILL REMAIN HERE, IN SAFETY...
NO. I WISH TO SEE HER AT BAY.
MIGHT NOT AN INHUMAN LACK OF FEAR CLOUD THE JUDGMENT ALSO?
AND WHAT NEWS FROM MECKLENBURG WAS DER MAGER MANN SO KEEN TO IMPART?
THAT IS OUTSIDE MISSION PARAMETERS.
OUR TARGET CAN FLEE NO FURTHER THAN THE ROOF. WE'LL INTERCEPT HER THERE.
IF YOU INSIST...
ACHTUNG, ALLE SCHLITTENTRUPPEN. TREFFEN SIE MICH AUF DEM DACH DER MOLOCH-MASCHINE...
PLEASE IGNORE MY COLLEAGUE'S MISGIVINGS. HE IS...
HE IS MORTAL. HE IS A MAN...AND THIS SHALL BE SETTLED BE-TWEEN WOMEN.

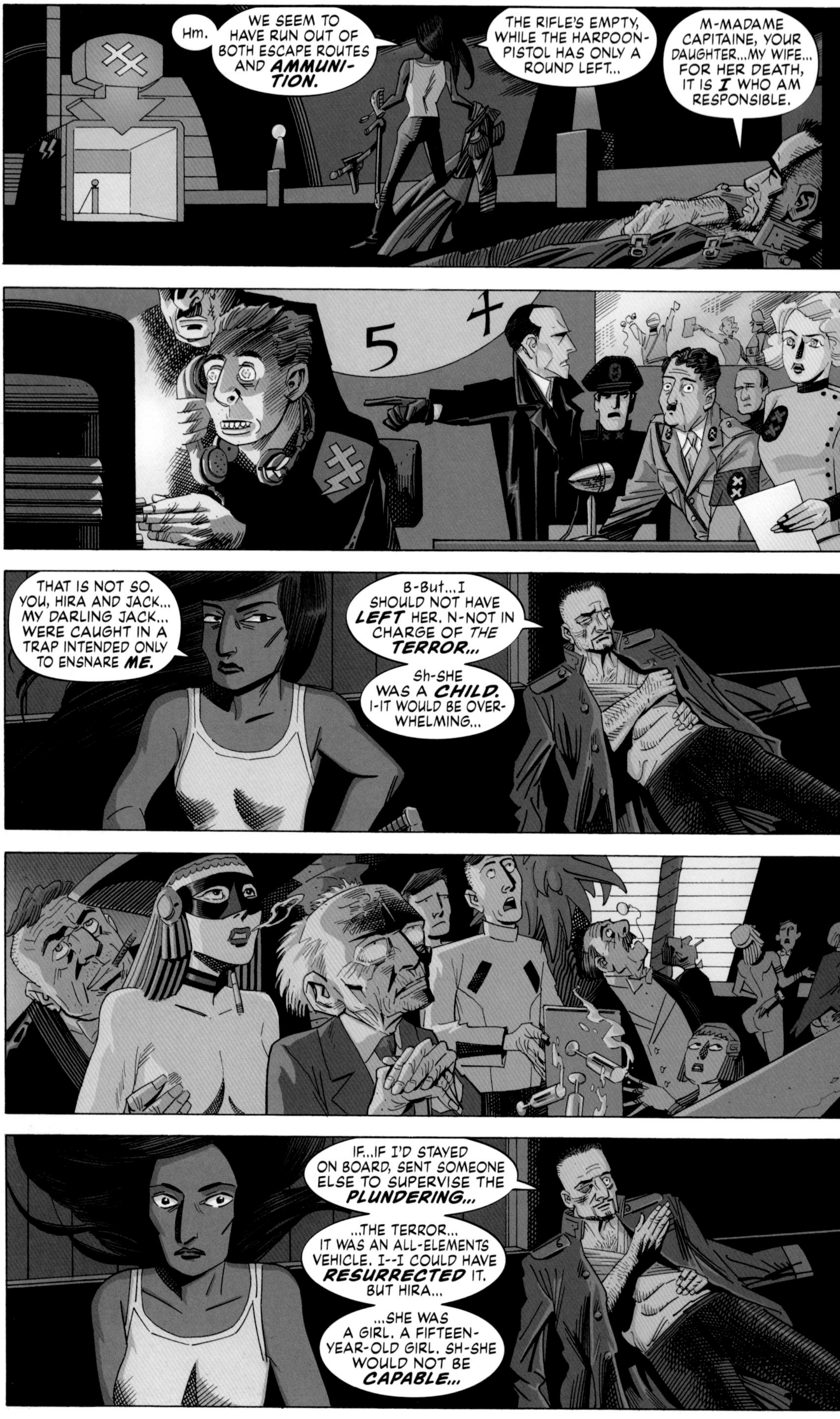
Hm.
WE SEEM TO HAVE RUN OUT OF BOTH ESCAPE ROUTES AND AMMUNITION.
THE RIFLE'S EMPTY, WHILE THE HARPOON-PISTOL HAS ONLY A ROUND LEFT...
M-MADAME CAPITAINE, YOUR DAUGHTER...MY WIFE... FOR HER DEATH, IT IS I WHO AM RESPONSIBLE.
5
THAT IS NOT SO. YOU, HIRA AND JACK... MY DARLING JACK... WERE CAUGHT IN A TRAP INTENDED ONLY TO ENSNARE ME.
B-But...I SHOULD NOT HAVE LEFT HER. N-NOT IN CHARGE OF THE TERROR...
Sh-SHE WAS A CHILD. I-IT WOULD BE OVERWHELMING...
IF...IF I'D STAYED ON BOARD, SENT SOMEONE ELSE TO SUPERVISE THE PLUNDERING...
...THE TERROR... IT WAS AN ALL-ELEMENTS VEHICLE. I--I COULD HAVE RESURRECTED IT. BUT HIRA...
...SHE WAS A GIRL. A FIFTEEN-YEAR-OLD GIRL. SH-SHE WOULD NOT BE CAPABLE...

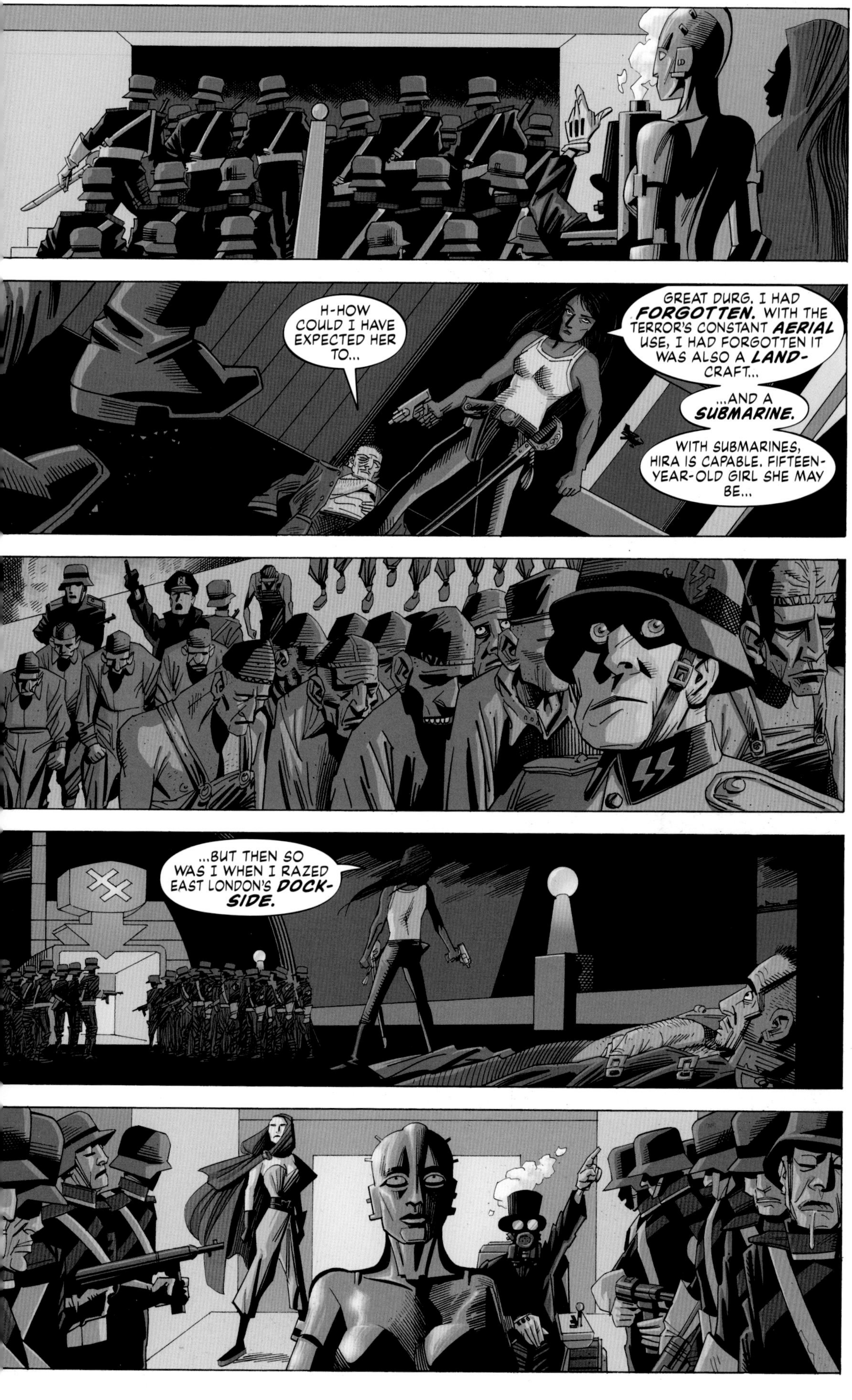
H-HOW COULD I HAVE EXPECTED HER TO...
GREAT DURG. I HAD FORGOTTEN. WITH THE TERROR'S CONSTANT AERIAL USE, I HAD FORGOTTEN IT WAS ALSO A LAND-CRAFT...
...AND A SUBMARINE.
WITH SUBMARINES, HIRA IS CAPABLE. FIFTEEN-YEAR-OLD GIRL SHE MAY BE...
...BUT THEN SO WAS I WHEN I RAZED EAST LONDON'S DOCK-SIDE.

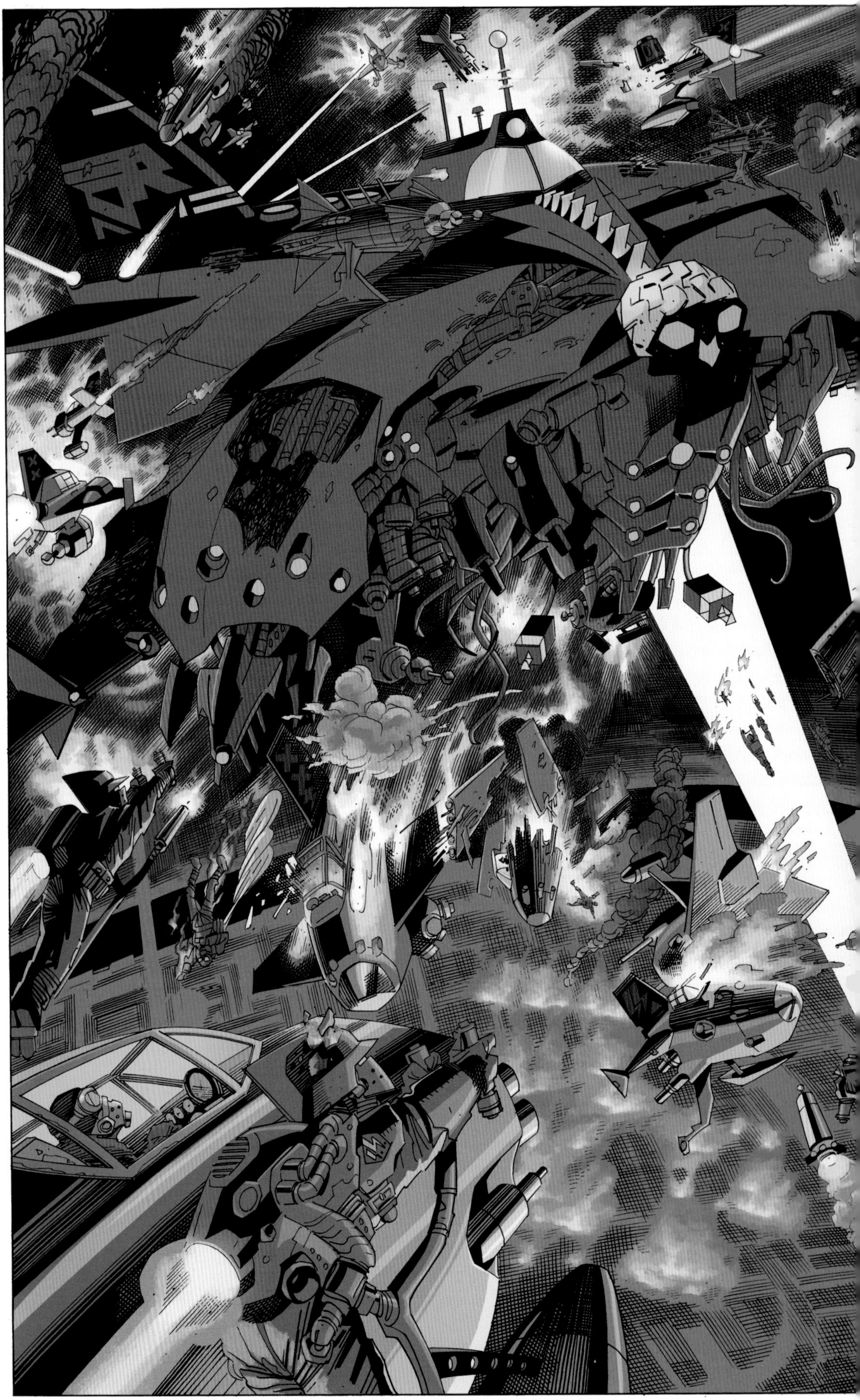

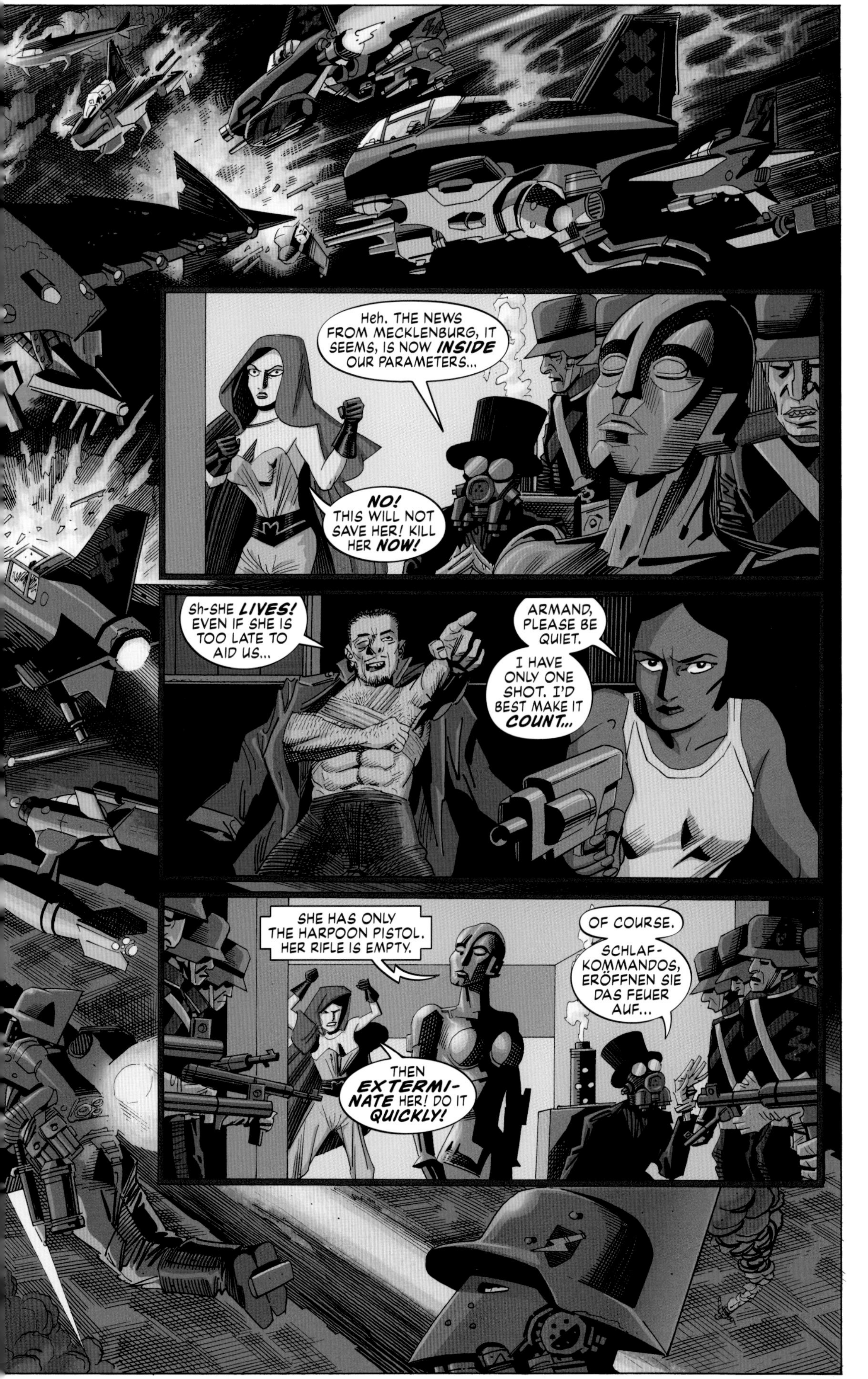

Heh. THE NEWS FROM MECKLENBURG, IT SEEMS, IS NOW ***INSIDE*** OUR PARAMETERS...
NO! THIS WILL NOT SAVE HER! KILL HER ***NOW!***
Sh-SHE ***LIVES!*** EVEN IF SHE IS TOO LATE TO AID US...
ARMAND, PLEASE BE QUIET.
I HAVE ONLY ONE SHOT. I'D BEST MAKE IT ***COUNT...***
SHE HAS ONLY THE HARPOON PISTOL. HER RIFLE IS EMPTY.
OF COURSE.
SCHLAF-KOMMANDOS, ERÖFFNEN SIE DAS FEUER AUF...
THEN ***EXTERMI-NATE*** HER! DO IT ***QUICKLY!***

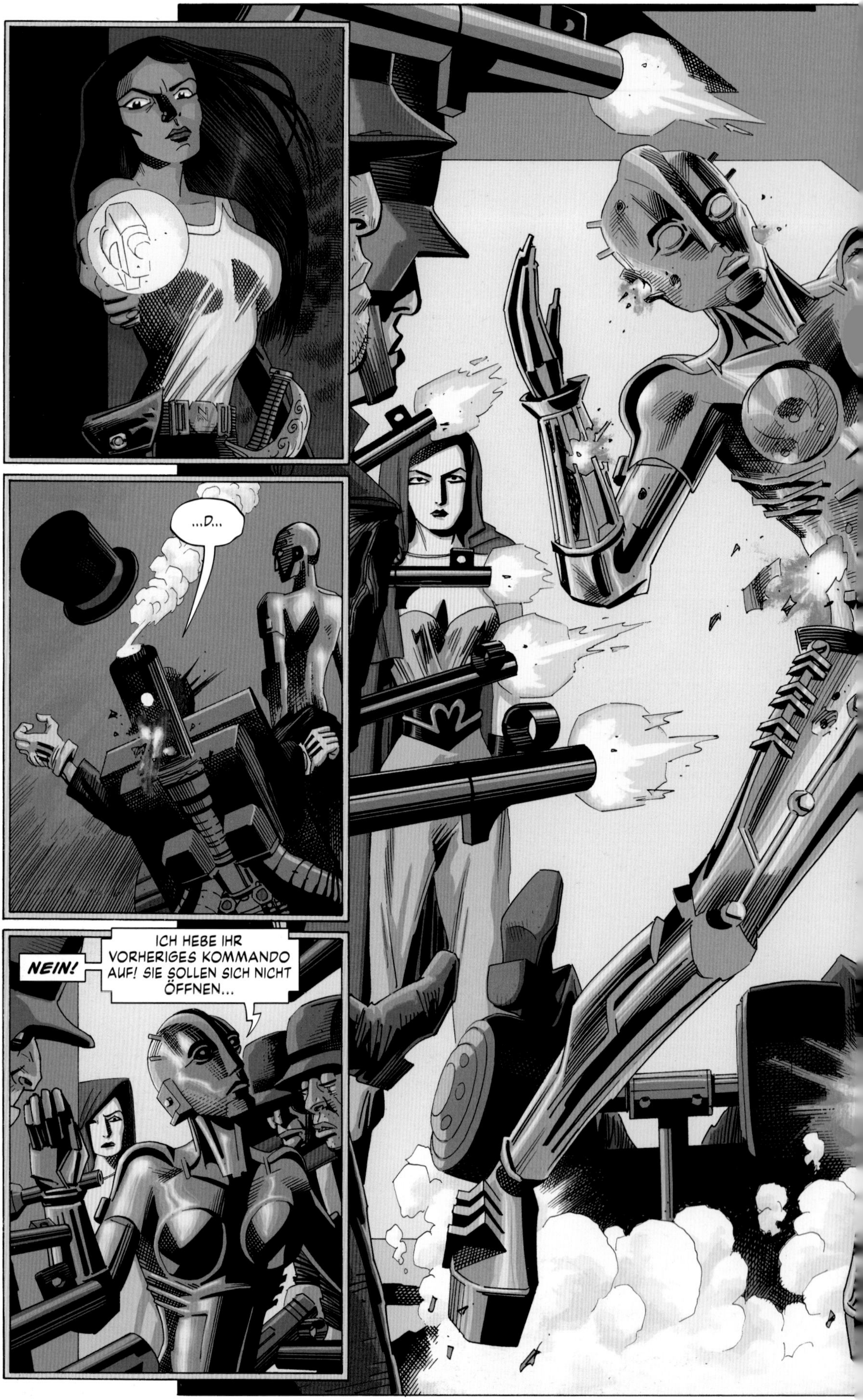

...D...
NEIN!
ICH HEBE IHR VORHERIGES KOMMANDO AUF! SIE SOLLEN SICH NICHT ÖFFNEN...

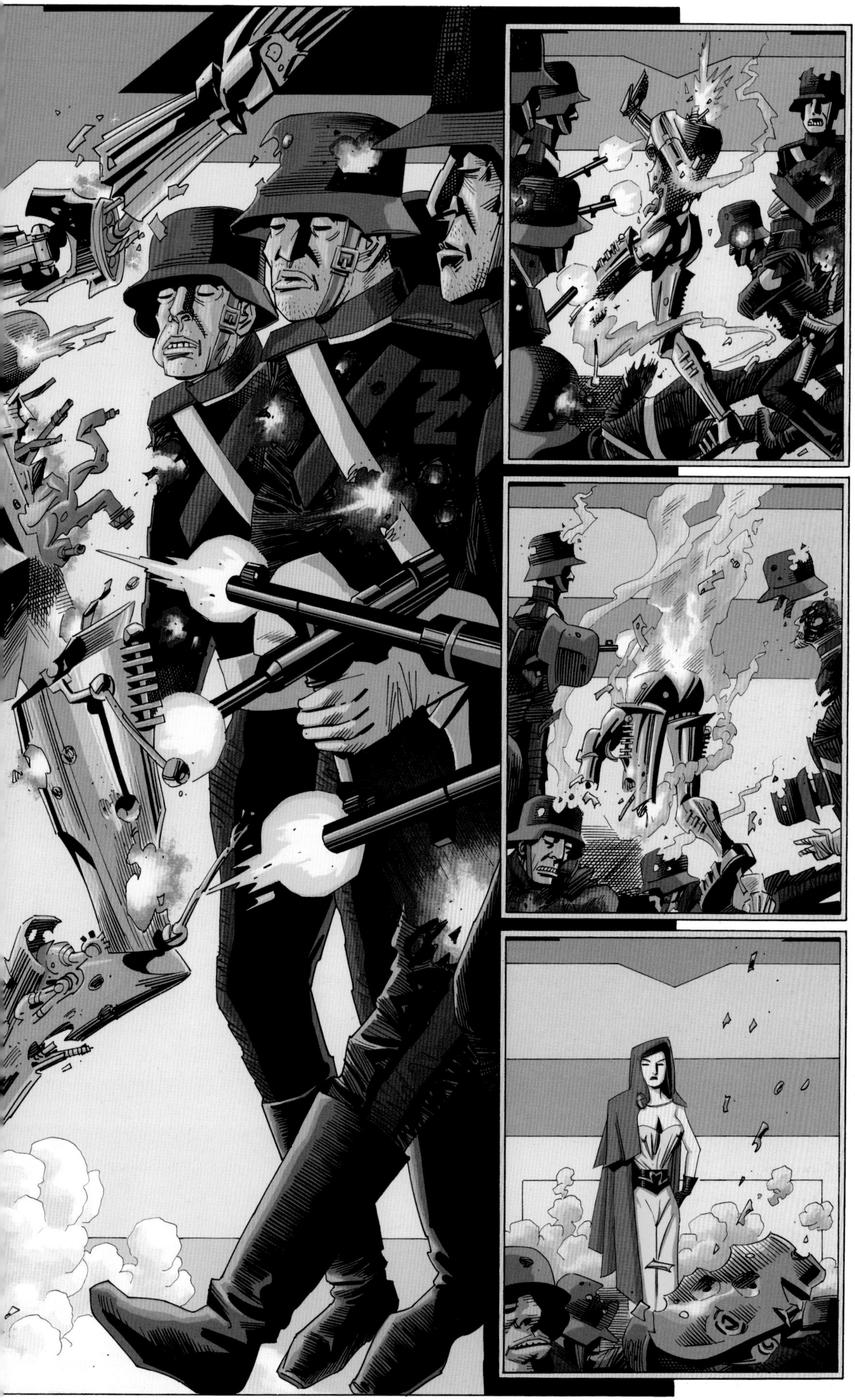

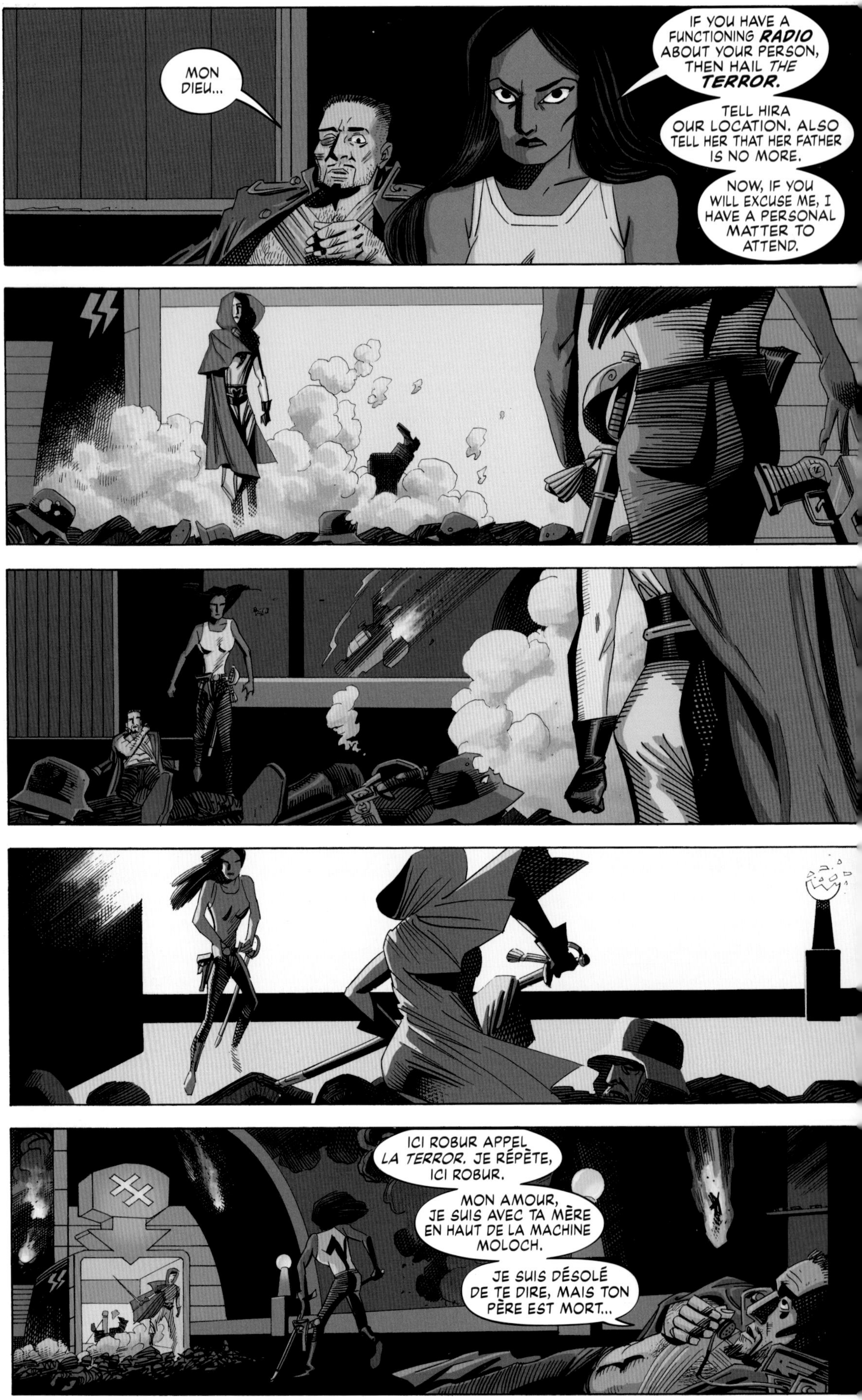

MON DIEU...
IF YOU HAVE A FUNCTIONING **RADIO** ABOUT YOUR PERSON, THEN HAIL *THE* **TERROR.**
TELL HIRA OUR LOCATION. ALSO TELL HER THAT HER FATHER IS NO MORE.
NOW, IF YOU WILL EXCUSE ME, I HAVE A PERSONAL MATTER TO ATTEND.
ICI ROBUR APPEL LA *TERROR*. JE RÉPÈTE, ICI ROBUR.
MON AMOUR, JE SUIS AVEC TA MÈRE EN HAUT DE LA MACHINE MOLOCH.
JE SUIS DÉSOLÉ DE TE DIRE, MAIS TON PÈRE EST MORT...

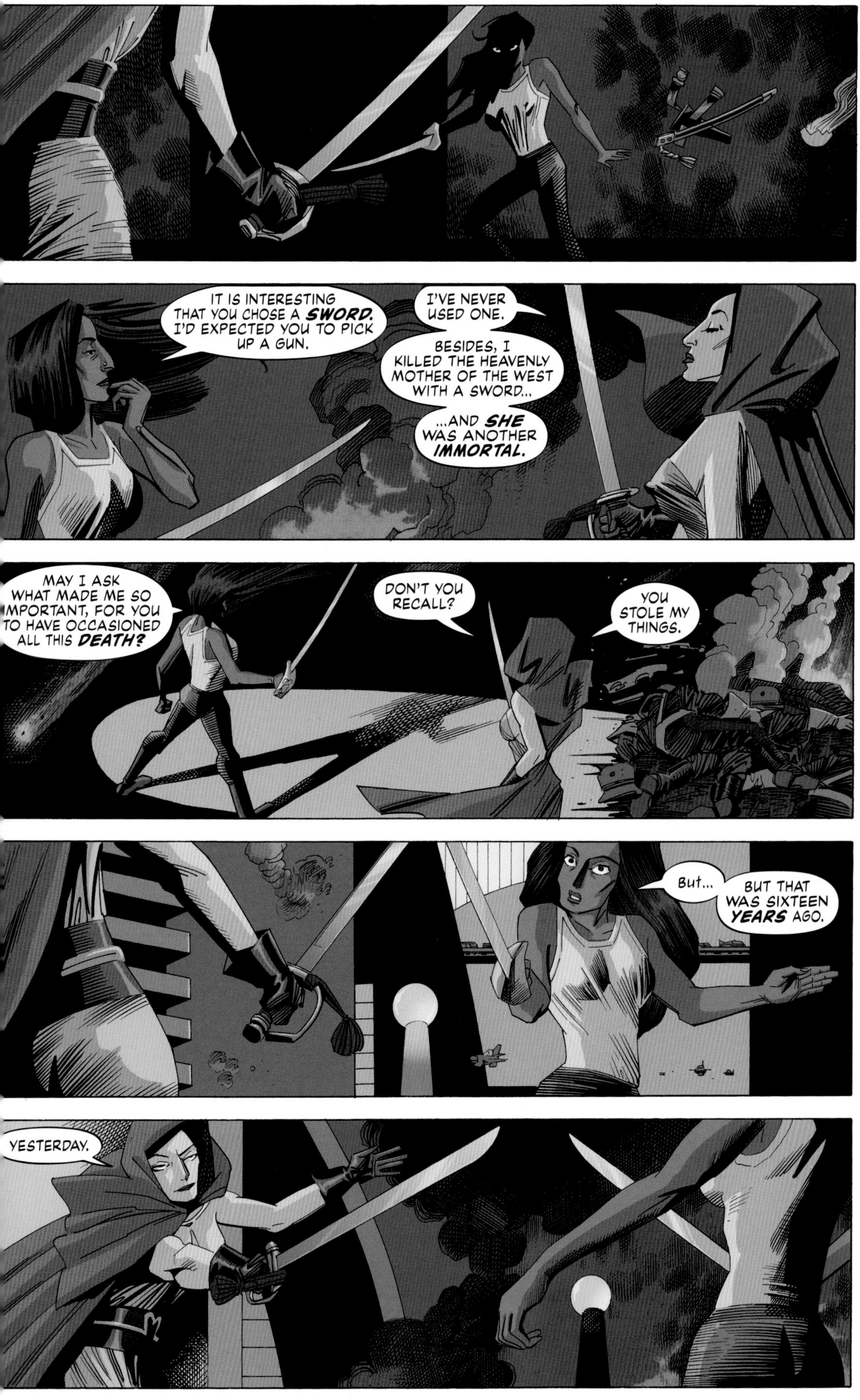
IT IS INTERESTING THAT YOU CHOSE A SWORD. I'D EXPECTED YOU TO PICK UP A GUN.
I'VE NEVER USED ONE.
BESIDES, I KILLED THE HEAVENLY MOTHER OF THE WEST WITH A SWORD...
...AND SHE WAS ANOTHER IMMORTAL.
MAY I ASK WHAT MADE ME SO IMPORTANT, FOR YOU TO HAVE OCCASIONED ALL THIS DEATH?
DON'T YOU RECALL?
YOU STOLE MY THINGS.
But...
BUT THAT WAS SIXTEEN YEARS AGO.
YESTERDAY.

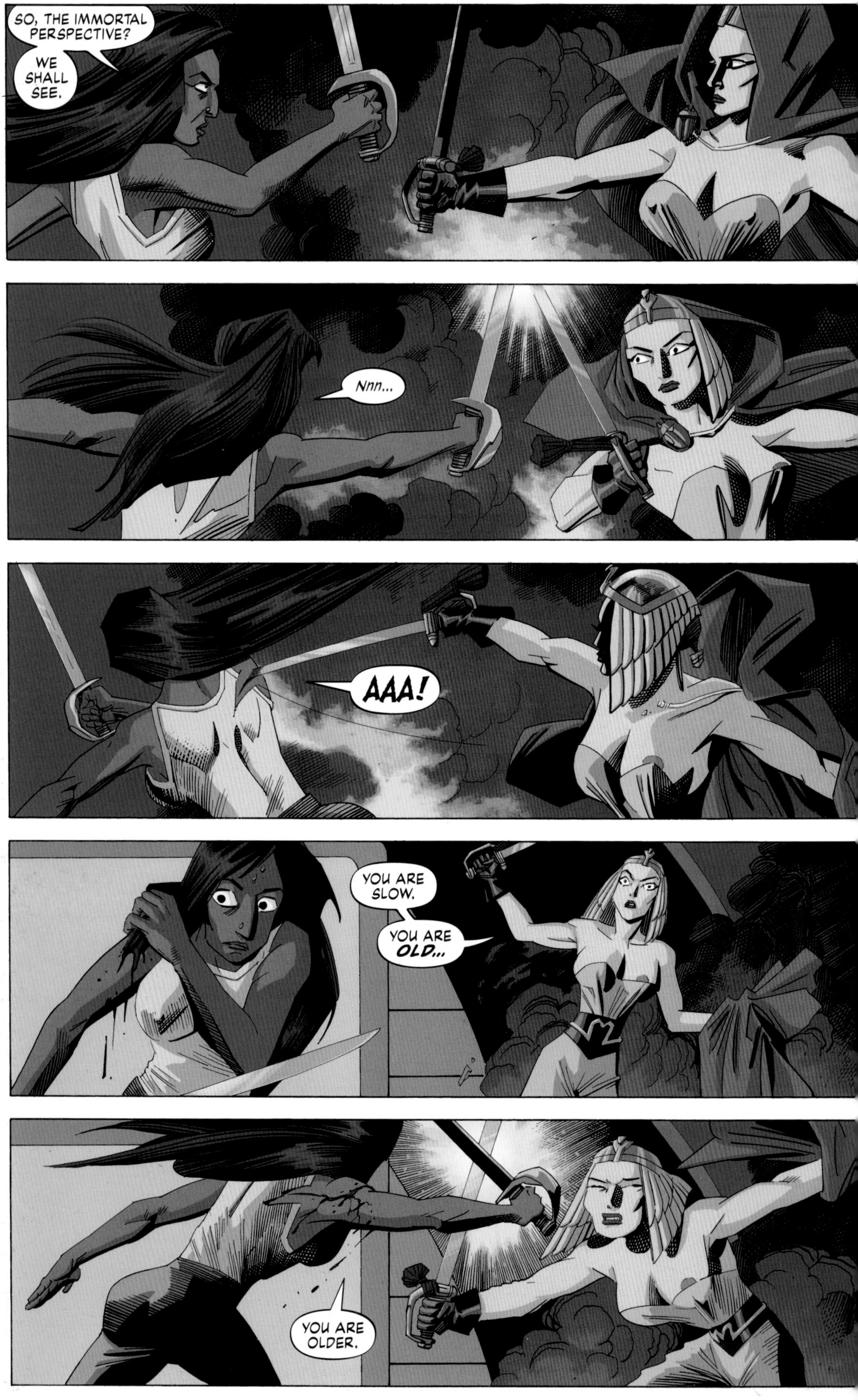
SO, THE IMMORTAL PERSPECTIVE?
WE SHALL SEE.
Nnn...
AAA!
YOU ARE SLOW.
YOU ARE OLD...
YOU ARE OLDER.

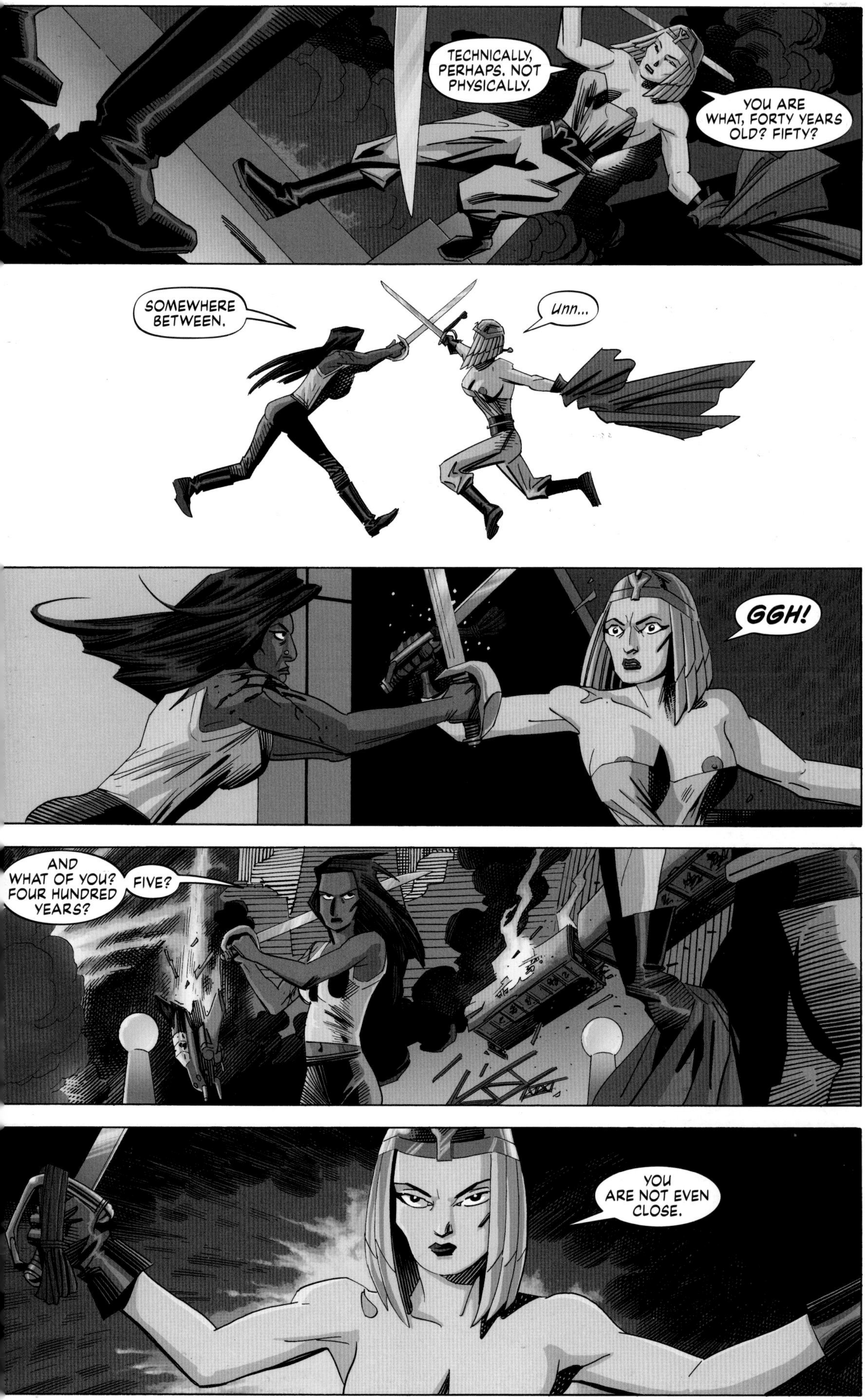
TECHNICALLY, PERHAPS. NOT PHYSICALLY.
YOU ARE WHAT, FORTY YEARS OLD? FIFTY?
SOMEWHERE BETWEEN.
Unn...
GGH!
AND WHAT OF YOU? FOUR HUNDRED YEARS?
FIVE?
YOU ARE NOT EVEN CLOSE.

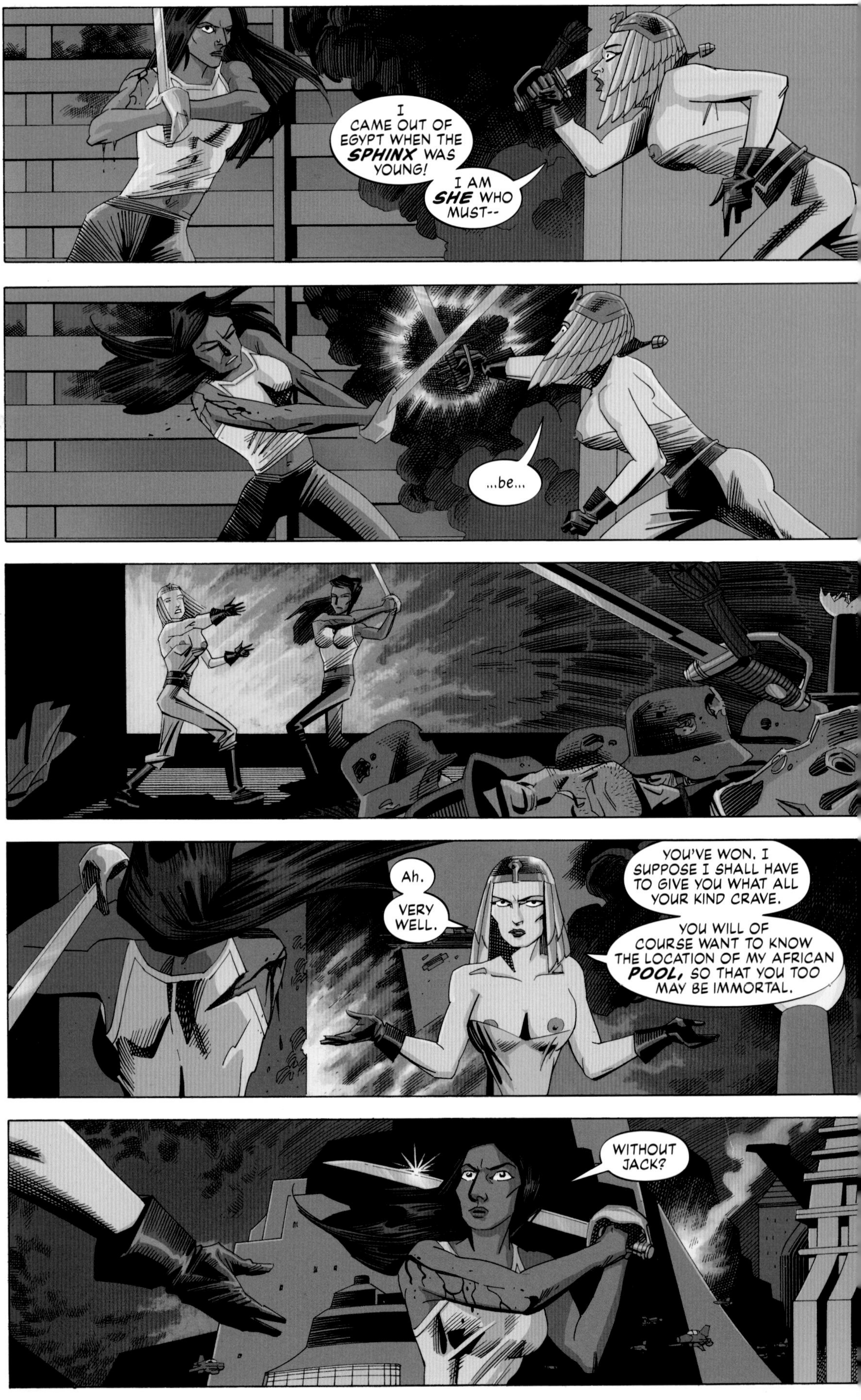
I CAME OUT OF EGYPT WHEN THE SPHINX WAS YOUNG!
I AM SHE WHO MUST--
...be...
Ah.
VERY WELL.
YOU'VE WON. I SUPPOSE I SHALL HAVE TO GIVE YOU WHAT ALL YOUR KIND CRAVE.
YOU WILL OF COURSE WANT TO KNOW THE LOCATION OF MY AFRICAN POOL, SO THAT YOU TOO MAY BE IMMORTAL.
WITHOUT JACK?

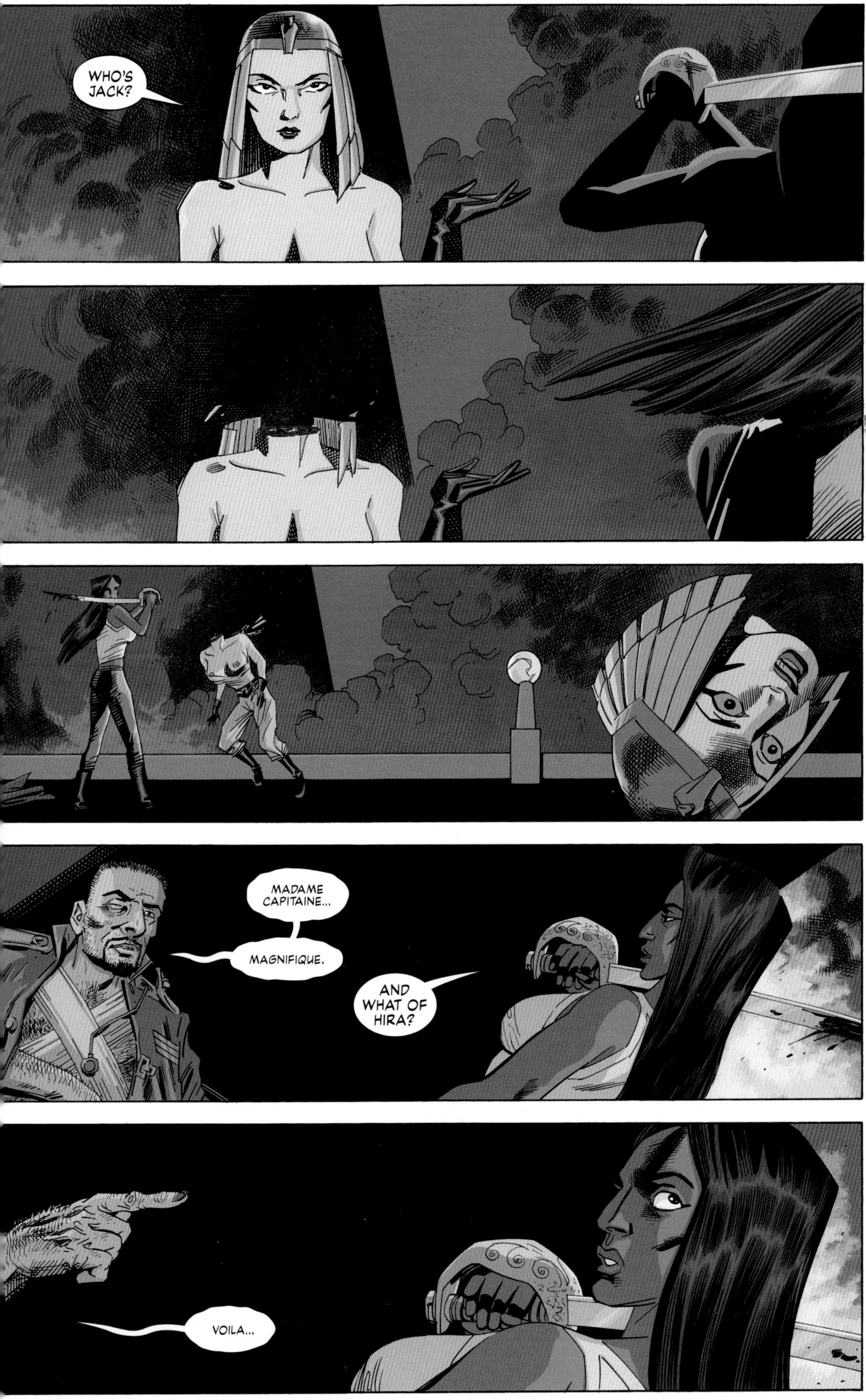
WHO'S JACK?
MADAME CAPITAINE...
MAGNIFIQUE.
AND WHAT OF HIRA?
VOILA...

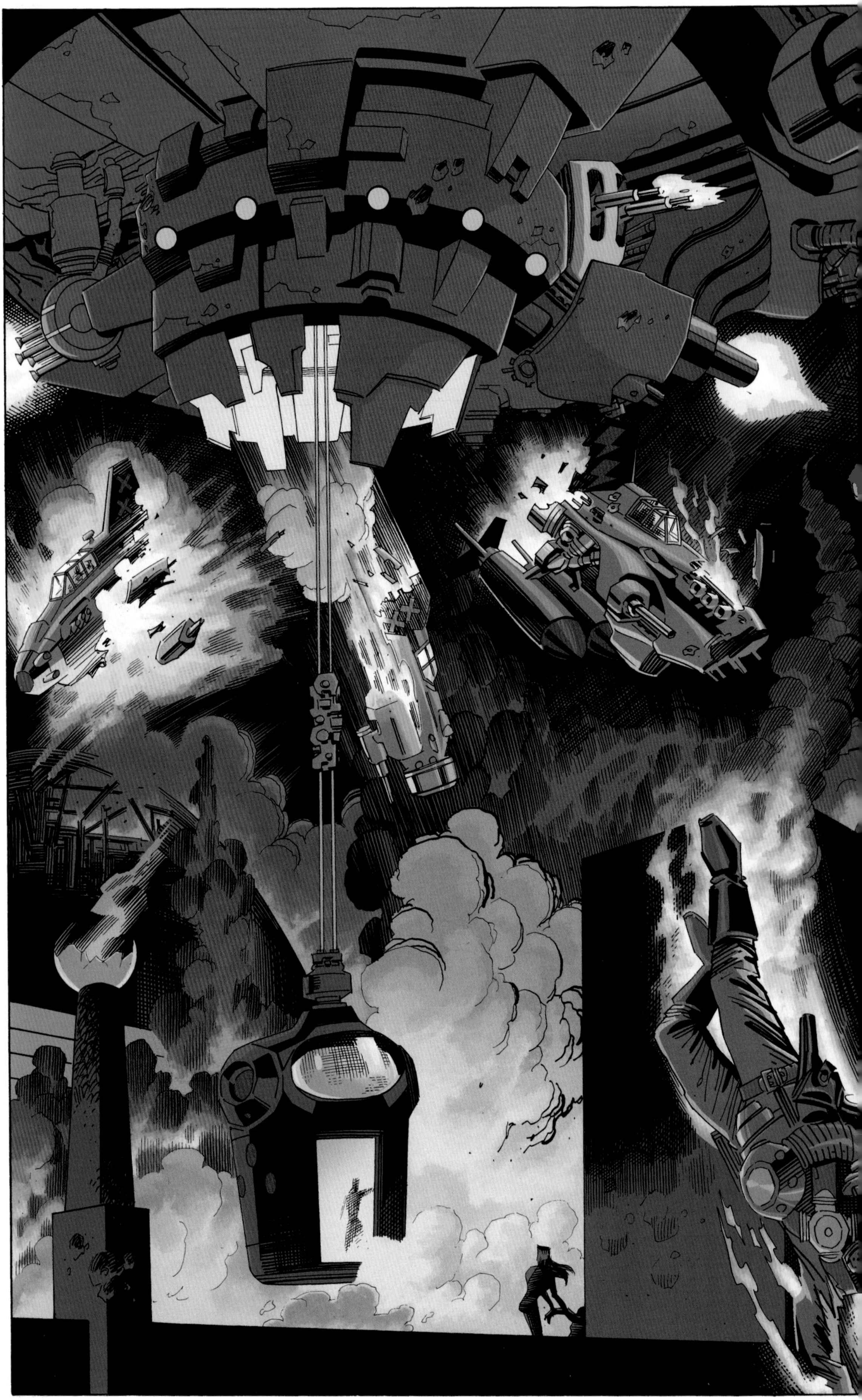

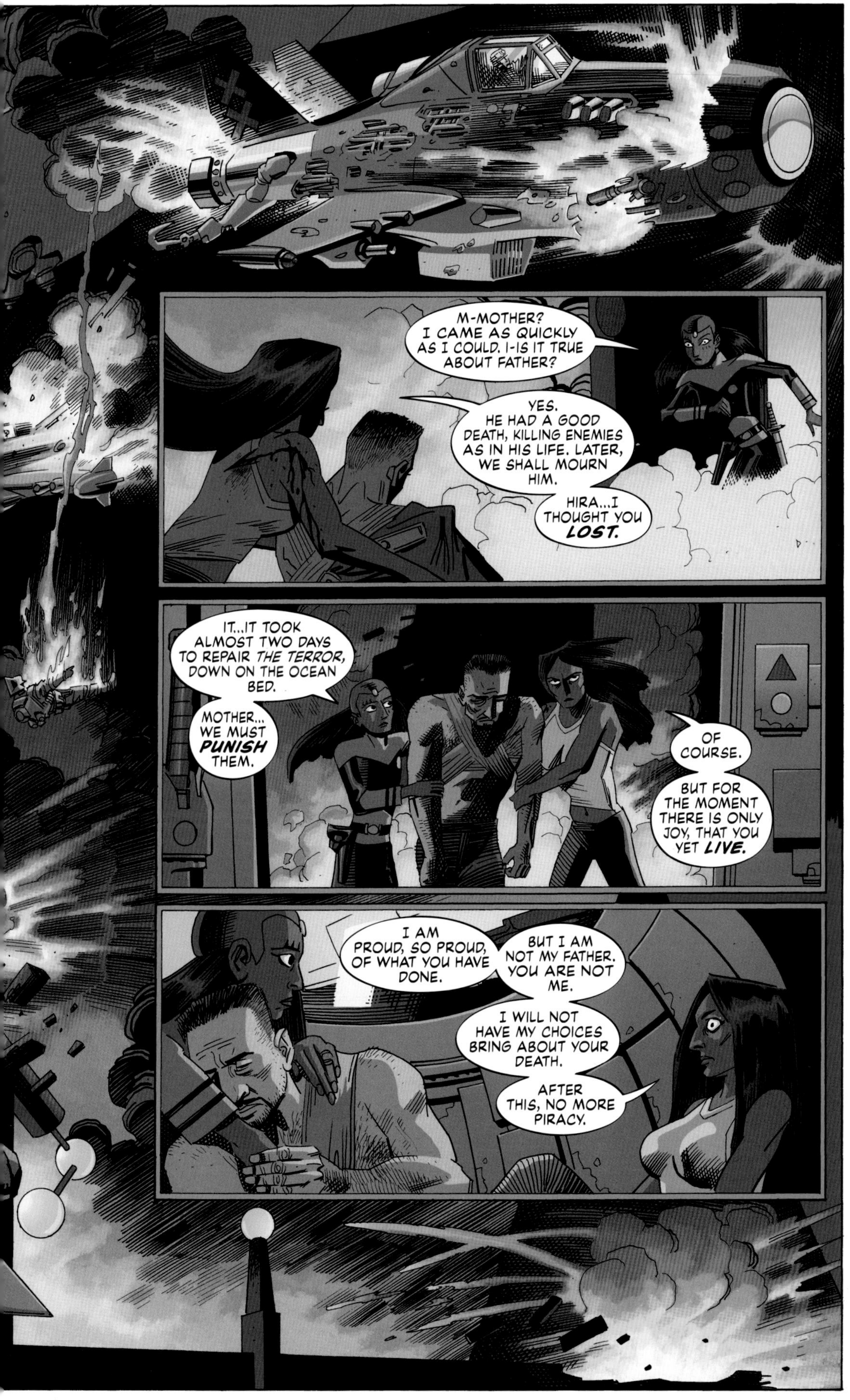

M-MOTHER? I CAME AS QUICKLY AS I COULD. I-IS IT TRUE ABOUT FATHER?
YES. HE HAD A GOOD DEATH, KILLING ENEMIES AS IN HIS LIFE. LATER, WE SHALL MOURN HIM.
HIRA...I THOUGHT YOU **LOST.**
IT...IT TOOK ALMOST TWO DAYS TO REPAIR *THE TERROR*, DOWN ON THE OCEAN BED.
MOTHER... WE MUST **PUNISH** THEM.
OF COURSE.
BUT FOR THE MOMENT THERE IS ONLY JOY, THAT YOU YET **LIVE.**
I AM PROUD, SO PROUD, OF WHAT YOU HAVE DONE.
BUT I AM NOT MY FATHER. YOU ARE NOT ME.
I WILL NOT HAVE MY CHOICES BRING ABOUT YOUR DEATH.
AFTER THIS, NO MORE PIRACY.

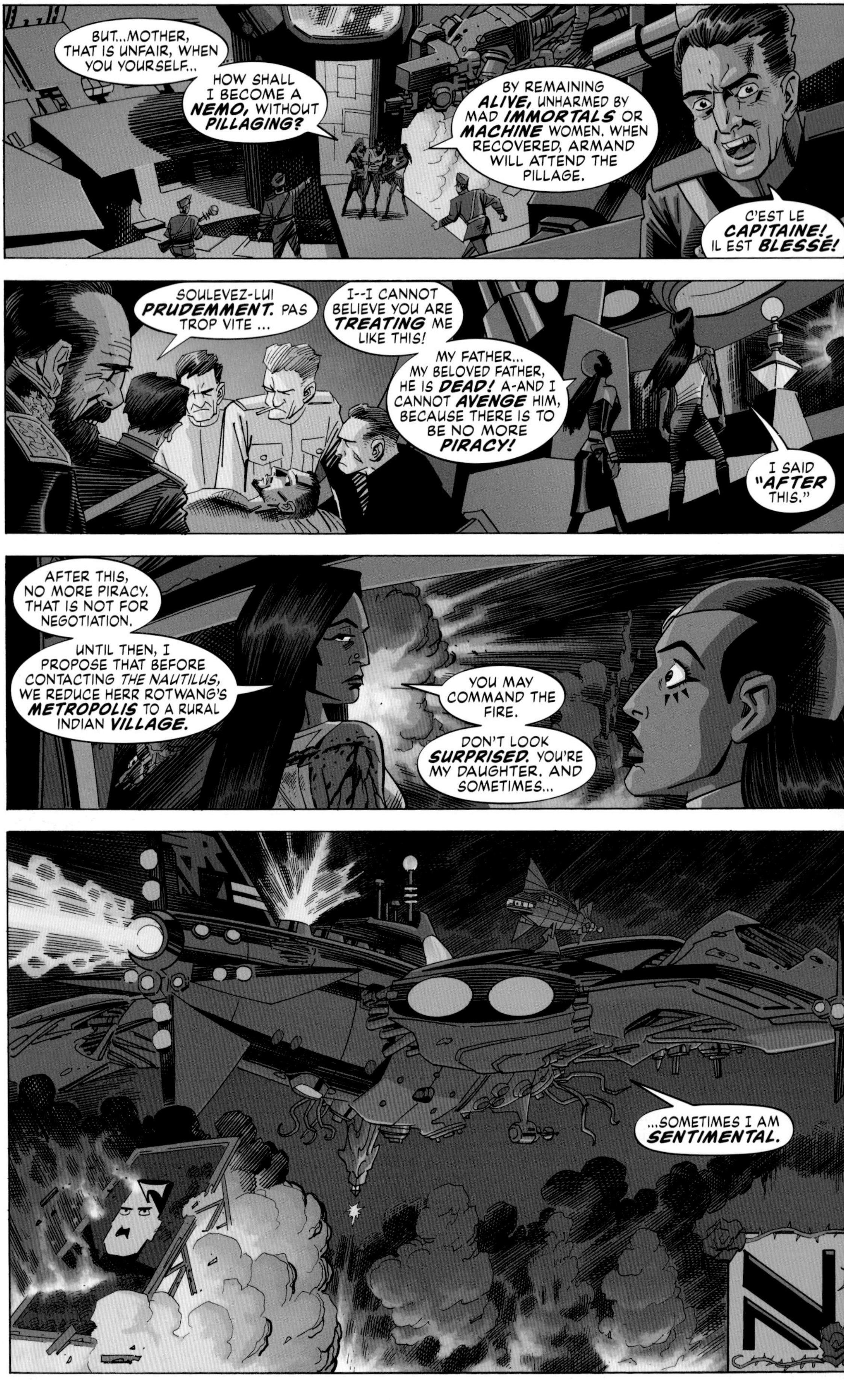

BUT...MOTHER, THAT IS UNFAIR, WHEN YOU YOURSELF...
HOW SHALL I BECOME A NEMO, WITHOUT PILLAGING?
BY REMAINING ALIVE, UNHARMED BY MAD IMMORTALS OR MACHINE WOMEN. WHEN RECOVERED, ARMAND WILL ATTEND THE PILLAGE.
C'EST LE CAPITAINE! IL EST BLESSÉ!
SOULEVEZ-LUI PRUDEMMENT. PAS TROP VITE ...
I--I CANNOT BELIEVE YOU ARE TREATING ME LIKE THIS!
MY FATHER... MY BELOVED FATHER, HE IS DEAD! A-AND I CANNOT AVENGE HIM, BECAUSE THERE IS TO BE NO MORE PIRACY!
I SAID "AFTER THIS."
AFTER THIS, NO MORE PIRACY. THAT IS NOT FOR NEGOTIATION.
UNTIL THEN, I PROPOSE THAT BEFORE CONTACTING THE NAUTILUS, WE REDUCE HERR ROTWANG'S METROPOLIS TO A RURAL INDIAN VILLAGE.
YOU MAY COMMAND THE FIRE.
DON'T LOOK SURPRISED. YOU'RE MY DAUGHTER. AND SOMETIMES...
...SOMETIMES I AM SENTIMENTAL.

HE JOHNSON REPORT:
Princess Dakkar of Lincoln

*ormer features editor **Hildy Johnson** makes a very special
*urn to these pages, tempted briefly from her well-deserved
*tirement to revisit old acquaintances on the occasion of the
*th birthday of the **Princess Dakkar,** known more usually as
*e second **Captain Nemo.***

They say that over time crocodile handbags will come
more closely resemble their owners, or perhaps it's the
*her way round. If I had a clear memory of anything pre-
*ding the beginning of this sentence I guess I might find
*at fact distressing but, as it is, what were we talking about?
*owever, not even the armour of senility or the shield af-
*rded by the ravages of drink could spare your formerly in-
*epid crone reporter from a confrontation with the passing
*ars when she was recently allowed a conversation with a
*milarly superannuated beauty, last encountered more than
*o decades before when we each counted several hundred
*en amongst our conquests, although in entirely different
*shions. Most of hers wound up as either dead or wishing
*at they were...but so did most of mine, now that I think
*out it from a vantage point of near sobriety.

My arrival on the shores of Lincoln Island, a long-
*nding pirate haven that is denied status as an indepen-
*nt country simply through its lack of postage stamps and
*rrency, was very different from that of my earlier visit
*ring, dear God, was it really 1938? On that occasion I
*d been transported from Chicago's waterfront directly to
*e island in my hostess's notorious submarine, the *Nauti-
-, whereas my current audience necessitated first a trip
*Argentina and a midnight rendezvous at a deserted air-
*ip outside Buenos Aires, which no doubt played merry
*ll with my arthritis. I was met by a delightful uniformed
*ung airman named Guillaume, one of the ailing Armand
*bur's 'Terrornauts', who then escorted me in a hair-rais-
*g aerial contraption that he called a 'zyomp-zyette' to his
*and base, as greatly altered since my previous excursion
*am I myself, although only in Lincoln Island's instance
*uld the alterations be perceived as an improvement.

In the silver drench of a full moon our craft began
*oaring drop towards the curdled masses of the Riallaro
*chipelago's famed fogbanks, billows parting like ethereal
*un sugar to reveal a startlingly space-age and electrically
*luminated view of Princess Janni Dakkar's brigand nation
*m above. The same eccentric (if not frequently phantas-
*goric) architectural forms that I had noted on my previ-
*s sojourn were still apparent, buildings shaped like manta
*s or swordfish or the like, but realised now in gleaming

new materials and decked with trailing jellyfish arrays of
burning bulbs and tropic tetra neon. This glittering citadel,
a cover illustration from the over-optimistic science fiction
periodicals of thirty years ago, rose to enfold us like a ba-
roque metal flower as we descended to the blazing ludo-
board of Lincoln's landing fields. Our steel-clad charging
rhino of a vessel touched down with the delicacy of a hum-
mingbird in the clearly adept hands of youthful Guillaume,
a display of skill eliciting a girlish flutter from my heart,
though luckily without the need for major surgery.

On disembarking I was taken (although sadly not by
Guillaume) for a walk across the airfield to my quarters in
the company of a strikingly tall and strong-boned Polyne-
sian girl of perhaps thirty-five years old who introduced
herself as one Luala Ishmael, seemingly the common-law
wife of the same Tobias Ishmael I'd encountered on my pri-
or trip to this cutthroat paradise. She told me in her perfect
if unusually-inflected English that her husband was now
old but in rude health, and that they quarrelled frequently
about the gender of the child both of them hoped for. "Mr.
Ishmael says that I must have a boy who will be strong and
take over his father's duties. I have said that if I have a girl,
it will be one like me, who smashed his teeth and put him
into the infirmary the night we met." Fervently hoping that
she wouldn't smash my teeth and put me through the fuss
of buying new ones, I made an attempt to change the sub-
ject by enquiring where the stupefying bulk of Armand Robur's craft the *Terror* that had dominated this expanse the
last time I was here was to be found. Luala's answer was
delivered in a tone of mournful resignation. "It is in French
Indo-China with its master. Mistress Nemo argued that his
health was very bad and that he could not help the situation
there, but Captain Robur felt it was a duty to his country.
No-one knows, now, when he will come back."

Reaching the guest accommodation that had been reserved for me, a single-story building artfully prefabricated
around what appeared to be a solitary turtle-shell of unbe-
lievable proportions, I bade a good evening to my chaper-
one after she'd forcefully impressed upon me that I was to
meet the Princess Dakkar the next day at noon at her "shark
palace". Somehow, I'd a feeling I would know this when
I saw it without need for supplementary directions. Once
Luala had departed and left to my own devices I discovered
the most sumptuous bunk I've ever had the fortune to be
offered; an enormous clam-contoured concavity brimming
with silken bedding and a brief note from Her Majesty grac-

ing the pillow stating that one of her crew would bring me breakfast on the morrow and that she herself looked forward very much to seeing me again. This was signed with the lady's customary 'N', an emblem better met with on dry land than glimpsed on an approaching flag during a rough Atlantic crossing. Thinking hazily about the many other persons who had set eyes on that ensign in less reassuring circumstances than myself I drifted without difficulty into a surprisingly deep and untroubled sleep, apparently less nervous amidst a healthy, thriving populace of cold-eyed ne'er-do-wells than in my own apartment. No need here to slumber with a gun at hand in the night table and, indeed, no point: the people here are consummate professionals who'd have your only-just-done scalp tied to their belts before you'd made your first move for the bedside drawer.

Dowager ruler of these territories, Janni Dakkar has changed both her island habitat and the essential methodology of her criminal enterprise since last we met, in those tense months before Adenoid Hynkel's military might invaded Poland, effortlessly crushing the already-tottering Ubu dynasty's regime and taking over the demoralised green candle industry. (I can still recall deposed King Stanislaw, Ubu the Third, and his heartfelt and eloquent denouncement of the German and Tomanian forces: "They are merdrers!") Having eagerly applied herself to plundering and sinking German vessels in the first years of that conflict, working in a pincer movement with her son-in-law, sky pirate Armand Robur and his ruin-raining craft the *Terror,* Princess Dakkar and her lifelong love Broad Arrow Jack found themselves lured into a slyly-baited death trap at the heart of Hynkel's Reich in the Berlin metropolis, a conurbation manifesting the cheese-dreams of infamous stranger-to-sanity, the happily defunct Carl Rotwang. Though a clear account of what occurred there in the German capital has never been made public, it is said to have involved the violent demise of most of Germany's still-active 'Twilight Heroes' that remained from World War I, and there are even rumours that African monarch Queen Ayesha met her end during the conflagration, with the current claimant to that title being no more than another mere pseudo-Ayesha such as have arisen on at least two previous instances during the self-styled goddess's uncommonly long life. What is a certainty, however, is that Rotwang's strange totalitarian city-state was comprehensively destroyed by Robur's *Terror* in the aftermath of those events, as we can also be entirely sure that Princess Dakkar's husband and the father of her child, Broad Arrow Jack, was a fatality of that mysterious episode.

After her husband's death, rather than giving in to grief the princess became a decidedly black widow, wreaking genuinely horrific vengeance on the Axis cause for the remainder of the war. It should be said, however, that in between bloody massacres the *Terror* and the *Nautilus* provided help and rescue services for many of the conflict's traumatised or displaced victims, such as Finland's relatively harmless and benign troll population after Russia's long, hard-fought invasion, or even their more vicious and belligerent near-relatives in Norway following the German and Tomanian conquest during April, 1940, when the Wehrmacht had been ordered to exterminate all troll-nests or cave complexes they came across "to the last suckling pup". With battle's end, the pirate queen intelligently managed to guide her piratical endeavour's smooth transition to the very different post-war world that was to come, diversifying into an efficient military force that have made several lucrative and notably successful interventions into global trouble spots throughout the later 1940s and the East-West

tensions of the 1950s. She was famously effective in h many strikes against the post-war U.S. communist admini tration of Mike Thingmaker (I can get quite nostalgic thin ing of those years when we saluted the red-white-and-r and cheered on Capitol Hill purges) and its ally in the 'B Brother' Ingsoc regime which flourished in Great Brita during the same period. This is not to suggest, of cours that Princess Dakkar is all through with piracy, but rath that she seems to have arrived at the conclusion that p litical and military machinations are a more sophisticat and remunerative application of the selfsame buccaneeri trade in which her family has traditionally made its livin In effect, Her Majesty has made the jump from being wha once referred to as a warlord debutante to her establishment an exponent of alarmingly well-armed rogue statesmanship

Upon awakening the morning after my airborne arriv on the island, I was unsurprised to learn that my hoste had been as good as her considerable word in having a d licious breakfast of exotic fruit and kedgeree delivered my turtle-shell abode. When this had been consumed ir voracious manner that would hardly be considered femini by any biped, I first showered by means of Lincoln's v canically-heated running water system, dressed, and th resolved that I should venture out of doors so that I h a chance to see by daylight the much-changed blackgua utopia before I kept my noon appointment with its monarc The peculiar structures of the central pirate township, w their decorative fins and tentacles made now from concre glass and gleaming metal served but to confirm my first ir pressions from the night before, namely that Lincoln Isla had embraced the modern world with such ferocity that had overtaken everybody else. Its populace were simila modified, at least in their appearance, although one suspe that in their basic nature they remained unchanged acr millennia, like alligators. Only the French ex-patriots w were attached to the divisions of the absent Robur wor uniform, and even that was managed with a certain raki informality. The rest of Lincoln's citizens, descended fr the roughneck crew of Princess Dakkar's legendary fath were of an encouragingly improved strain, seemingly le afflicted by the signs of syphilis or scurvy than their fo bears and with fewer wooden legs, eye-patches and pr thetic hooks upon display, making it all in all much easier keep one's curried fish and kiwi down. It struck me that twenty years the progress made in hygiene, health and sa ty standards had done much to make the islanders a mo formidable and deadly fighting force while at the same tir making them appear more civilised as individuals. To honest, I think I preferred it when a pirate could be rea ily identified by virtue of his being a monocular multip amputee who spoke exclusively in the present imperfe While I'm sure that Blackbeard had his flaws and may times have been socially clumsy, at least everyone kne where they stood, even if they had fewer legs to stand or

Finding the Shark Palace, as I'd earlier supposed, p sented little difficulty. Once I'd spotted the colossal w dow-studded fin that sliced into the balmy sky above all the island's other buildings, it was pretty much plain saili I located the main entrance by the decorously understa and not even slightly vulgar giant squids which curv about its archway, and within the soaring lobby area w once more greeted by the flinty-eyed and muscular Lu wearing what appeared to be a holstered Luger pistol at hip, a detail that I hadn't noticed in the darkness that tended our first meeting. Somehow both engagingly pol and yet obscurely threatening, the gold-skinned giant

companied me to glass-sided elevators on which, not to
overdo the maritime motif at all, particularly spiteful-look-
ing lobsters had been etched with acid. It occurred to me
that we were only short an elevator operative dressed as a
flounder, though conceivably I might have called on his day
off. Arriving at the top floor I was shown into an elegant
suite of seemingly endless rooms, with in the furthest such
high-ceilinged chamber Princess Dakkar and her intimates
awaiting my arrival.

Iron-grey hair bound in a turban and her well-cut emer-
ald military jacket dropping almost to the top of her black
boots, the princess gave a smile of recognition as I entered,
one leathery predator acknowledging another. There were
three younger persons stood about the criminal aristocrat,
with only one of them that after a few moments' scrutiny I
could identify as Princess Dakkar's daughter Hira, whom
I last met on her wedding day when she was twelve years
old. Now an astonishingly beautiful young woman in her
middle thirties, clad in a translucent purple sari with a seven
month-old baby cradled in her arms, the younger princess
asked after my patently precarious health and introduced
me to her infant son, named Jack for her late father. While
near-incandescent with the joys of motherhood after so
many years in the attempt, she nonetheless retained a look
of strained anxiety no doubt occasioned by her frail, mal-
aria-prone husband Armand being presently at risk in the
uncertain heavens of French Indo-China. The other person-
ages present, who'd been offering their birthday salutations
to the elder Dakkar prior to my arrival, turned out unexpect-
edly to be a brace of Germans. Ursula Mabuse (everyone
calls her Uschi, it would seem) is an attractive woman in
her fifties and apparently the daughter of the late Dr. Mabuse, the ruthless mastermind behind the Weimar under-
world who had enjoyed friendly relations with the House
of Nemo since the 1940s. The handsome young man also
in attendance, dressed immaculately in what looked to be
a Prussian variation on the standard Robur uniform, was
Manfred Mors, a grandson of the famous 19th-century German Luft-Pirat who'd had family condemned to labour
camps by Hynkel and was now acting commander of the
still-substantial Robur forces left on Lincoln Island. For-
mal handshakes once exchanged, the trio – or quartet if
one includes the baby – graciously allowed Luala to escort
them to the elevators leaving me alone in the unnerving
presence of a person voted recently as third in a poll listing
enemies of mankind in the 20th century, immediately after
T.H.R.U.S.H. and SPECTRE, armed with nothing save for
rudimentary Pitman's shorthand. We talked with unprec-
edented informality for perhaps twenty minutes and I was
surprised to find myself greatly enjoying this extraordinary
woman's company. Eventually, I was permitted a short interview, which I now reproduce below.

Hildy Johnson : So, how would you summarize the
seventy years that you're celebrating?

Princess Dakkar : (LAUGHS) Only with difficulty. Lots
of screams, some of them mine back in the earlier days but
less so later on. Or possibly it is best summed up as a lesson
in how the determination necessary to avoid resembling an
overbearing and fanatical parental figure is precisely that
figure's unique, defining quality. I have become my father
in all save his beard and his abiding catalogue of grudges
dating from the Indian Mutiny, an incident I cannot feel as
passionate about as he did.

HJ : And do the memories stay with you? I find I forget
so much...

PD : Then you're a lucky woman. I recall it all. I can
recall the smell of London's docksides all ablaze, and even
something of what we discovered in Antarctica. The stench
of the decaying giant ape that we transported to Skull Island for a decent burial is with me still, as are the dreadful
intonations of the machine-woman I encountered in Berlin.
Beneath this coat there are burns on my arm caused by the
radioactive exhalations of the huge bipedal saurian with
which the *Nautilus* engaged some several years ago in wa-
ters off Japan, and I remember yet annihilating nests of vari-
ous extra-planetary species or prodigiously-sized nuclear

mutants that were manifesting in America throughout the brief Thingmaker government's regime and afterwards. But there are memories, too, which are a consolation. I recall the wheezing chuckle of my former first mate, Mr. Ishmael, a man more a father to me than my own, and above all I am unable to forget the precious years I spent with my beloved Jack, when we were king and queen of all the planet's blood-soaked billows.

HJ : That's a romantic image. Any memories of your father you can bear to keep around?

PD : There is his skull, fixed to the fo'c'sle of my *Nautilus,* which I believe serves adequately to preserve him in my thoughts. No, that is callous, and dismisses someone of that stature far too readily. It was the fire in him, for better or for worse, that forged me, and I have long since come to acknowledge that. I sometimes talk with him, you know. He is among my ghosts.

HJ : Your ghosts? Am I to take that in a literal sense?

PD : Unless we have a workable idea of what ghosts literally are, then who can say? Once Jack and I took Hira to Spectralia, where there are phantoms of the sort one reads about in the accounts of Silence or Carnacki. They are not of the same kind I often have about me now. Perhaps, more plausibly, the spirits that by turn afflict or entertain me are but consequences of an ageing mind and memory that slides into decline. Jack is too seldom with them, or I would not make complaint.

HJ : So does this ghost train mostly haul a freight of victims? Isn't that what some of us would call a conscience?

PD : (LAUGHS) No, not at all. I think I recognise my conscience on those rare occasions when I meet with it. The apparitions I describe are somewhat different. Not all of them are what you would refer to as my victims, although certainly that faction is well-represented.

HJ : What of Queen Ayesha? There were rumours that the two of you were far from best friends, and I wondered if she might be in your ghostly entourage of...former combatants, let's say.

PD : I seldom think about her since I killed her in Berlin.

HJ : I've certainly heard rumours and reports to that effect, although with someone of that nature I'd have thought that there must always be an element of doubt...

PD : Then you are incorrect. I cut her head off, more than twenty years ago.

HJ : Really? I'd not heard that. But what about the current claimant to the throne of Kor who says that she's Ayesha? Don't you think that...?

PD : I beheaded her. She's dead. Now, if you'll pardon me I must make preparations for my birthday celebrations later on this evening, to which you are cordially invited. I shall summon Mrs. Ishmael to escort you down. It has been pleasant meeting you again, and I...ah! Here's Luala now.

And that was that. I nervously attended the princess's birthday party later, where I danced with the most courteous Manfred Mors, although I fear his major purpose was in keeping me away from Princess Dakkar with whom I'd apparently hit something of a sore spot in my interview. Later that night Luala walked me, no more than a little tipsy, to the landing field where to my great relief she neither smashed my teeth nor put a Luger round between my eyes but instead handed me to Guillaume for the zyomp-zyette zyourney back to Argentina. Here amongst the dubious home comforts of Chicago a week later I still find I'm thinking of her, not without a certain measure of affection. In that spirit, here's to Janni Nemo, seventy years old a week ago and still by far the world's most dangerous grandmother. Long may she sail, but not near any boat that I'm around. □

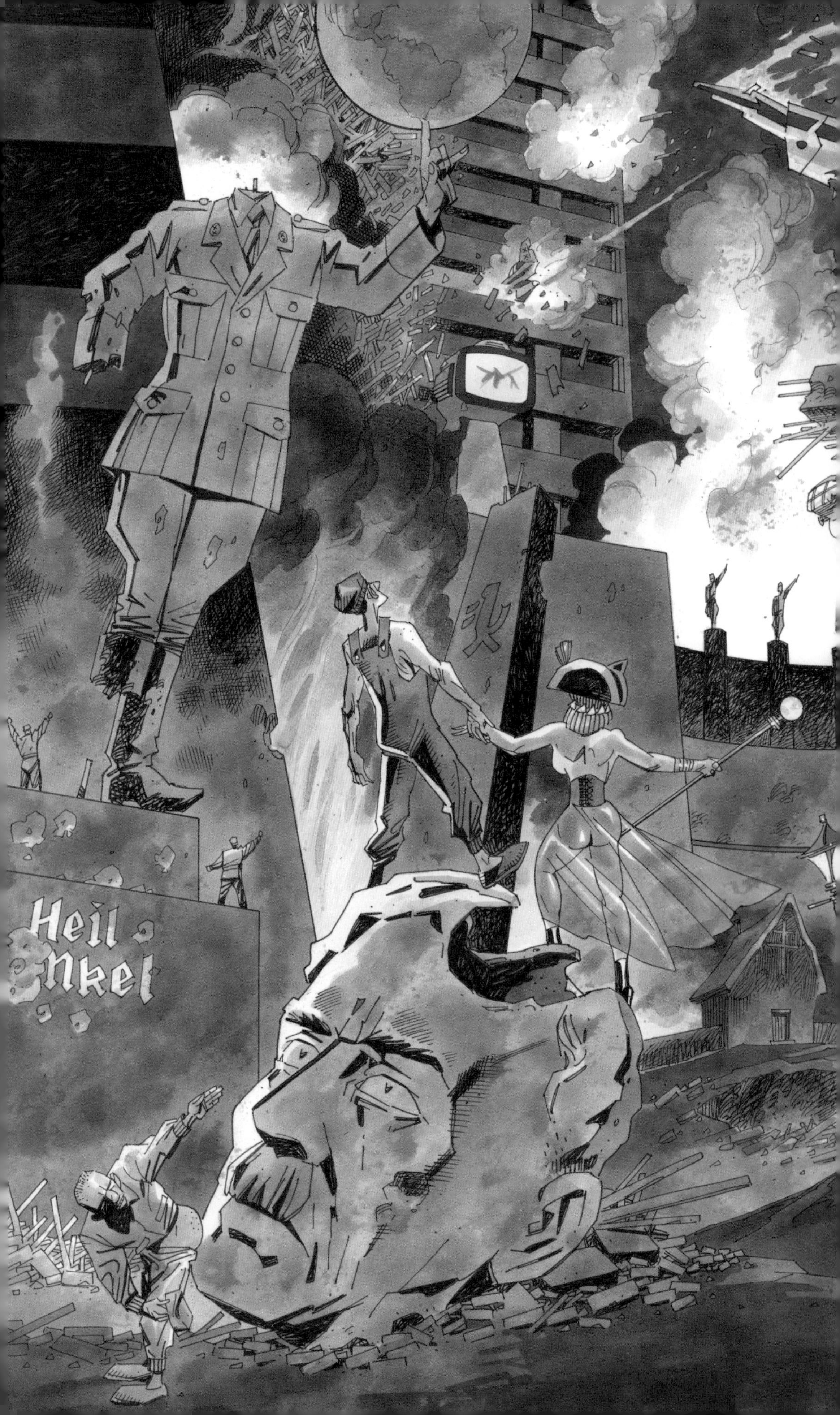
Heil
nkel